Praise for God Spelled Backwards

A beautiful, at times heart-breaking, and ultimately heart-warming story by a woman doing the tough work in animal rescue. The world needs more people like author Sylva Kelegian.

Teresa J. Rhyne
New York Times Bestseller of "The Dog Lived (and So Will I)"

A fascinating and beautiful story about animal rescue told with grace and honesty.

Alison Eastwood
Actress/Director/Animal Advocate

Bravo to the brave and enlightened actress, Sylva Kelegian, who teaches us through her powerful words that we all can be "human doings" and not just human beings. Her riveting, page turning account of life in the trenches of animal rescue, will make you both laugh and cry. The reader is perched on her shoulder as she rescues dog after dog, often putting herself in danger - all for her love of animals, and the belief that they should be treated with dignity.

Linzi Glass
Critically acclaimed Author/UCLA writing instructor

This is a must read encyclopedia on how to be a great dog rescuer. Sylva and I have saved many lives together, some of which you can read about in GOD SPELLED BACKWARDS.

Eldad Hagar
Hope For Paws

Thank you, Sylva Kelegian, for this powerful account of the tender, suspenseful, frightening, infuriating, inspiring world of dog rescue. A breathtaking journey about souls among us who give humans boundless adoration and love, drawing us closer to the creator of all life. A real page-turner! This book should be sold at every shelter and pet store in the country.

Jennie Redling
Award Winning Dramatist

GOD SPELLED BACKWARDS

GOD SPELLED BACKWARDS

The Journey of an Actress into the World of Dog Rescue

Sylva Kelegian

Print information available on the last page.

Sammy & Sylva Cover Photo: Michael Brian

Rev. date: 09/22/2015

To order additional copies of this book, contact:
Xlibris
1-888-795-4274
www.Xlibris.com
Orders@Xlibris.com
541327

CONTENTS

PROLOGUE

I remember riding the subway in my mid-twenties while reading about New York City's Center for Animal Care and Control in *New York Magazine*. The article talked about how many dogs and cats were euthanized every year, month, week, and day. The numbers were staggering, and the description of conditions in the shelter was shocking.

I was not focused on animals at the time and had none in my life since leaving home, but the feeling I had after reading that piece was that I had peeked into a hidden world. It seemed like a secret the public had been unaware of until now, and most likely did not want to be aware of. It was a horrible secret that made me feel helpless on the deepest level.

I put the story out of my mind. After all, there was nothing I could or really wanted to do about it.

Years later, as I was running around Los Angeles rescuing dogs from the streets, protecting animals from neglectful homes, and saving them from shelters, I remembered that article and wondered if it was some kind of omen. Was I meant to read it back then? Was it a glimpse into what I would be dealing with in the future? Maybe it was the universe saying: *Ready yourself. You will feel a calling that will shake up your world. You will save innocent lives from death row and find them loving homes. It will be emotionally rewarding, extremely challenging and push you to your limit, but* **you** *will be an animal rescuer. And though crushing on the mind and heart, your soul will have a purpose, and your life will be worth living.*

CHAPTER ONE

A New Life

Should I stay in Los Angeles or go back to New York? I prayed. *Give me a sign.* I was an actress. A struggling one. LA had not been good to me. But then again, I had not been good to myself either, and it was time for that to change.

The next morning, I stood in the middle of the street outside the Hollywood YMCA looking down at the piece of newspaper in my hand. The cars drove around me honking their horns. I was frozen in awe. I had only stopped to pick up the paper to recycle it when I got home, as I didn't like to see litter on the street. It was April 1995, and in my hand was the *New York Times* Arts and Leisure section, dated February 22—my birthday.

It was the sign I needed.

I was on a plane back to New York the following week.

The decision was the right one. I had finally learned to ask God for help, and my life changed.

Two years later I was engaged and no longer struggling. My fiancé, Jude Ciccolella, was a successful New York actor; I had become a working one, starring in independent films, Off-Broadway plays, and guest starring on the *Law & Order* television dramas. And though I didn't realize at the time how ironic it would turn out to be, I shot a commercial with Michael Vick for ESPN.

Jude and I met at the Actors Studio the year I moved back and fell in love while rehearsing a scene from the play *Jackknife.* "Oh, wouldn't it be great to have a dog!" I crooned to him one warm sunny day as we walked in Riverside Park. A couple nearby, having a picnic, looked so happy with their Golden Retriever snuggled up beside them. "A dog would give us something to take care of." I was not ready to have children, but my heart had been opened and it was time to love a dog, as well as a man.

"Absolutely. Once we're more settled," Jude agreed.

I gazed out at the Hudson River that day and thought, *Wow, I can't believe I'm here on a beautiful Sunday afternoon with my fabulous fiancé, strolling in Riverside Park, talking about getting a dog.* Before I left LA, I had made a promise to myself and to my girlfriends who had watched me suffer for so long: *I will no longer fall in love with unavailable men.*

The majority of the previous years had been spent in agony, not feeling worthy of being loved. This, coupled with a terrible case of acne in my twenties, sent me into a deep depression. "You're really talented, but with your skin I'm afraid it will be hard to get you any TV or film jobs," a top agent told me. He had seen me in a play when I was starting out and had called me in for a meeting. His face dropped as I walked through the door. "You should stick to theater. You can't see it on the stage," he gently informed me.

After Jude and I were married, I had a longing inside me. Not to just be comfortable with my new life but to do something to help others, since I was now "okay." I then asked God to *use* me in some way.

I began by mentoring an eleven-year-old from Harlem who was having a hard time with her mother and needed some guidance. The girl knew she was gay, but her mother would not accept it until years later. We spent many weekends together exploring Manhattan and talking about life, and it was during that time I was pointed in a direction I never dreamed possible. Jude was working in Los Angeles on a TV pilot while I was rehearsing a play in New York. On the wall of the dressing room was a sign asking people to walk a rescue dog at a local vet's office. I remember reading that posting and getting a flurry in my gut. The possibility of extending myself to an animal thrilled me. I felt ready to take care of something, even if it was just for an hour walk.

The following day I showed up at the vet's office. "Hi. I'm here to walk Annie, the small Pitbull mix," I said with a smile on my face. "There was a sign up at . . ."

The young man behind the desk stopped me. "Annie got a home yesterday," he said. "One of the volunteers adopted her."

"Oh." I felt deflated after gearing myself up to be of service.

"But we have a puppy you can walk, if you want. She's finally strong enough to go outside."

"Sure. That's fine. That's great," I said, as I felt myself filling back up.

The young man reached for the phone. "Can you put Sammy on a leash and bring her to the front? Someone is here to walk her."

I sat down in the waiting room and stared up at the second floor landing where he said the dog would be coming from. A few minutes later she appeared, and I got up to greet the five-month-old strawberry blonde Shepherd/Corgi puppy stumbling down the steps. I will never forget that long journey down her first flight of stairs and how Sammy bounded over to me when I knelt to greet her. Her ears were too big for her small body, and her tail was longer than she was.

"No one has ever walked her," the vet tech told me. "She was brought in a few weeks ago, extremely emaciated. The irresponsible owners left their six-year-old in charge of feeding her. He never did." The tech rolled his eyes. "Our IVs kept her alive, and now she's healthy enough to be adopted."

After a week of me walking Sammy and trying to adopt her out to good people in the dog park, I met a guy who I thought would be perfect for her. "I'll bring my wife to the vet's office to meet her tomorrow," he said, after witnessing how well she played with his dog.

My friend Janet, who was contemplating getting another pet, also came to meet Sammy that day but was on the fence about making the commitment. "No worries. Think about it. The guy in the park seems great, and I hope he comes through tomorrow," I assured her.

Janet didn't miss a beat. She had obviously been mulling over what she was about to tell me: "She's meant to be your dog. She looks like you and she acts like you," she said. "You have the same color hair. She's petite and feisty. You are supposed to adopt her. She's your dog."

On the way back to the vet's office, my friend's words beat on my brain like a jackhammer. I knew she was right, but I had not come to a place where I was ready to *adopt* a dog . . . yet. I was just getting my feet wet walking one. Sammy made eye contact with me as she trotted on my left. We had become very close in the last week, but I was doing my damnedest to keep my guard up.

It took me years to commit to a man, and now being faced with the reality of having a dog, I didn't know if I was ready. By the time we got back to the vet's office, I had come to a decision. I knelt beside her before we entered. "I will take you home tonight," I said. "If you let me sleep my eight hours and then if they don't come for you tomorrow, I will adopt you." Her deep brown, soulful eyes met mine, and she cocked her head to one side, then the other. It was a deal.

The guy at the dog park had been so great. I was sure he would show up with his wife the next day. I felt safe knowing I would not have to live up to my commitment. I told the young man at the vet office that Sammy would be coming home with me that night. The following morning, after she *had* let me sleep my eight hours, I brought her back.

All afternoon I was torn, wanting to find her there when I returned and at the same time, hoping she had been adopted. At ten minutes to five p.m., before the vet office closed, I walked in the door and took a deep breath. "Hi, Marilyn," I said to the vet's wife who ran the rescue group. "Is Sammy here, or did someone come for her today?"

Marilyn was a great gal who adored all dogs, especially Pitbulls, of which she had many. "No, Sylva, no one came. I really wish you—"

"I will," I interrupted. "I'll adopt her. She's mine. She's supposed to be mine." I told Marilyn about my plan, the pact I had made with Sammy the day before. I paid the fee, filled out the adoption and microchip paperwork, and ordered an ID tag.

My Princess, as she would later be known, was now mine, and my world was about to change . . . drastically.

CHAPTER TWO

Adventures of a New York City Canine Princess

Sammy and I settled into our new life together in New York without any problems, aside from the first week when she growled at me while I was eating my dinner. My puppy had been starved in her old home, and she wanted my food.

"Turn her over on her back, hold her down, and tell her *no*," the trainer said when I called.

After I did my best alpha imitation, my hand shaking from fear of hurting her or being bitten, she never growled at me again. Instead, she would lie and wait until I was done eating, when she was allowed to lick my plate.

My husband Jude returned home the following month and fell in love with her as well. His feelings were greatly tested when the two of them were in the Catskill Mountains that summer at a friend's house, and a family of bears sauntered in through the back door. Jude, not wanting to alert the bears, stayed low and quietly held Sammy tightly against his chest, trying to comfort her as she panted heavily from fear. "I felt really good. I realized I would have put my life on the line for her," my husband said proudly. Thankfully, the mama and babies left out the back door before he was forced to be a hero.

My world had opened up. In the same way the lives of women who have children become centered on their kids, their kids' friends, and other mothers, my life was now revolving around my dog, her friends, and their owners. As I got to know all the four-legged children in our group, I realized every one was different, just like us. Each of them had distinct personalities, likes and dislikes, just like us. They felt joy, sadness, and anger, just like us. They expressed themselves verbally, just like us. They had their favorite friends, just like us. The only difference was that they spoke a different language, and could not care for themselves without our help. And they loved unconditionally. I knew from that time on, I would never live another day without a dog.

Every morning at seven and then again at four p.m., my new companion and I would meet our friends in Riverside Park for an hour of play. On most afternoons, while I was out, Sammy's best friend Lucy—a joyful, yellow Labrador Retriever—would come and stay in our apartment. Or my Princess would go to her apartment, or Max and Judy's, or to the apartments of Mabel or Wags, her other dog friends.

Sammy's favorite thing to do was chase sticks. We had an area of the park that we called *stick stadium*, and she would run back and forth after the sticks, out of her mind with excitement, as Jude or I threw them.

I had never felt the kind of love I was now feeling for my dog. It was maternal love, and in my mind, she was my four-legged daughter, the female love of my life, with all the concerns that come along when loving someone that much.

My fears were tested one afternoon when she walked into the elevator without me. Not knowing the elevator was standing open on our floor, I let go of her leash to lock the apartment door, and by the time I turned around, she was gone. Panic set in. I was told that a dog had died when his leash got caught in the elevator and he had been hanged as the bottom dropped. I ran down twenty-three flights of stairs, faster than the elevator. Not knowing what I would find, I was shaking as the door opened and a man walked out. "Is that your dog?" he asked, as he gestured inside. There, in the back left corner, where I had taught her to sit while riding, was my Princess. If she had not gone to the back of the elevator, the next story would not have happened, as she would most likely have died that day.

I had taken her out to do her business at eleven p.m. We had the same routine that time of night: walk fast out the front door of the building and go straight ahead to the curb. Within moments, Sammy would relieve herself, and within five minutes of leaving our warm apartment, we would be back in bed. But this night took a bit longer, as the "thing" that came out of her made me stand in shock as people walked by and gasped. She pooped a large, gray, hard mass that looked like it should have come out of a horse. We went back upstairs with the plan to go to the vet first thing in the morning. However, at four a.m., when I got up to pee and was on the toilet, Sammy came into the bathroom and sat in front of me. It was dark, but I could see from the moonlight coming through the window that something was not right. When I turned on the light, my Princess was a different dog. Her face was so swollen she looked like a chow. "Oh my god! Sammy, what happened?" I cried. But her new appearance and that bowel movement said it all. Something had poisoned her. I threw my clothes on, and we raced off in a cab to the East Side 24-hour vet.

I paced, like any worried mother would do, while they ran tests. It was finally decided that Sammy was allergic to the red, green, and yellow dyes in her kibble. I immediately found a natural food for her, and the problem went away.

Not long after that scare, I left Sammy at the apartment of her friend Wags for a play date while I went shopping. Wags, a Golden Retriever, lived across the street and had a very sweet but non-dog-savvy parent. As I approached my apartment building with my grocery bags, a neighborhood dog walker came running up to me. "Your dog was hit by a car and ran into the park!"

"What?!" I screamed.

"She was playing with Wags on the sidewalk, his owner dropped her leash, a truck backfired, and she bolted!"

I dropped the bags I was carrying and ran toward the park. I was panicked. I had never felt such fear before, but I remember consciously thinking this was a test of my faith. I stopped, calmed myself down, and prayed. "Thank you, God, for leading me to Sammy. Thank you for not letting her be hurt, and thank you for leading me to her." Then, breathing deeply, I started running through the park calling her name.

Ten blocks later I saw a park ranger and asked him to take me to the park's office to use the phone. I called my answering machine, with the hope that someone had found her and called the number on her ID tag. The first message beeped, "Hi, I found your dog in the batter's box at home plate in the Seventy-Second Street baseball field. She had her leash on. It was the only way I could get her because she was scared. We're now in the dog park on Seventy-Second Street. I hope you get this message soon, but if not here's my number."

I lived on Ninety-Second Street and was now on Eighty-Sixth Street.

"He found her! They have her!" I screamed. "She's at the dog park on Seventy-Second Street!"

"Well, let's get you there then!" the park ranger exclaimed as I ran and got back into his truck.

When we approached the park, I jumped out of the truck. My Princess saw me and immediately came running toward the gate. "Yay! Yay!" The people in the dog park were clapping as Sammy jumped into my arms. The guy who found her came up to me, and I gave him a big hug, with tears streaming down my face.

"She's not hurt?" I asked, as I looked her over.

"She doesn't seem to be. Why?"

I told the gathering crowd that she had been hit by a taxi and traveled over twenty blocks, which made them even more thrilled that we had been reunited.

"Here, have this," I said, as I handed the guy fifty dollars. Luckily, I had my small purse draped across my body with the strap on my shoulder, or I would have dropped it with the groceries. "I can give you more tomorrow." He looked like he could use some help.

"Wow, thanks, but that's good enough. I'm just happy I found her."

"I'll meet you here at the same time tomorrow and give you some more," I offered.

"That's cool. This is more than enough, really. I'm just happy she's okay." And he meant it.

"Well, you're a good guy. Thanks. And thanks, everyone! I'm going to get her to the vet, in case something internal is going on." The dog lovers stood at the gate, watching and waving as we drove away. I felt like I was in a movie.

It was against policy for the ranger to take his truck out of the park, but he was concerned about my Princess as well, so he drove us the eleven blocks to the vet.

"She's just fine. Not a broken bone or scratch on her," Marilyn's husband, the veterinarian, said. "Probably propelled off the bumper."

I put my arms around Sammy and gave her a big kiss. "You scared the hell out of me, young lady," I whispered, as she let out a sigh. "You're one lucky girl."

That night my dog slept soundly, until she woke me up running in her sleep.

The day's experience made me realize how much Sammy and I loved each other and how many good people were out there . . . . Later, I was to discover how many *bad* people there are as well.

CHAPTER THREE

The Riverside Stray

It was early on a hot July evening in the summer of 2001. The last rays of the sun were streaming into the window of our West End Avenue apartment. I had just taken Sammy out to relieve herself and was about to jump into the shower and wash off the sweat and grime from running around the city all day. My Princess followed her mama into the bathroom and stared at me, cocking her head to one side. "All right, let me feed you first," I said to my highly intelligent, impatient canine. Then the phone rang. A call from my husband and the night changed instantly.

"Sylva, I'm walking on Riverside and 110th Street, and there is a dog running around here. He's going to get hit by a car. Can you come?" Jude was known to walk up to ten miles a day. It was his way of working out, mentally and physically. There was an urgency and concern in his voice that I had never heard before. He was now a dog lover.

"I'll be right there!" I said loudly.

I remember the feelings that came over me: excitement, fear, an adrenaline rush. I didn't realize it then, but I would come to know that emotional state very well in the following years, whenever I got a call to rescue a dog. But this was the first time. I grabbed a leash, some treats, and ran out the door, leaving Sammy to wonder when she was going to have dinner.

I hailed a cab, and within five minutes I saw my husband in the distance. At the same time, I also noticed a 35-pound black Terrier running around the grassy median and a cop car sitting nearby. I threw the money into the front seat to compensate the cab driver. "Thanks!" I said as I jumped out and ran toward the dog.

"Is he yours?" the cop called out.

"No, I'm trying to help him. Can you help me get him?"

"No, we don't catch strays. Sorry."

Wow!

I had never rescued a dog from the streets and had no idea how to do it. Sometimes life lessons are learned the hard way. The first thing that I did wrong was to chase him. Canines can run faster, and you will never catch them. I realized later that, in order not to appear confrontational, I should have gotten on my knees with my body sideways and held a treat in my hand for the Terrier to see. If that didn't work, I should have followed him slowly.

By now, the dog was heading toward the stairs, leading down to a lower level that connected to the freeway. As I ran after him, I called to Jude, "They won't help. I'm going to get him!" The Terrier was running very fast. I increased my speed even more, trying vainly to catch up with him. Jude couldn't cross the street because of the traffic. At the bottom of the stairs, I saw the dog run toward the locked gate of a parking area, where he stopped. As I came toward him, he turned around and looked into my eyes. He was scared. He didn't know I wanted to help him, so he bolted around me, up the freeway ramp. "NO!" I screamed and ran after him. When he got to the top and saw the cars, he turned around and headed back toward me. I looked in his eyes and called to him, "Come on, boy."

What I should have done was walk back down without looking at him, so that he could follow safely. But in my naiveté, I didn't. Instead, I scared him even more. He turned around and ran onto the freeway, and a moment later I heard brakes locking, tires screeching, and a loud thump. By the time I made it up the ramp, cars had slowed down, swerving to avoid running over his dead body. I think I screamed. I was shaking. I started to run toward the dog, but someone grabbed me. It was a man who had seen us on the ramp and pulled his car over. The police showed up within five minutes, not the same ones who hadn't helped before. I was crying, and they put me in the back of their car to calm me down. A dark-haired, stern, thirty-something cop said, "You're lucky no person was killed." Then he left me alone with the air conditioning and radio.

As I watched the cops remove the Terrier's body, I felt like I was in the Twilight Zone. Only fifteen minutes ago I had been in my apartment about to feed Sammy and take a shower. Now an animal was dead, because of me. Lee Ann Womack's song, "I Hope You Dance," came on the radio, and I remember listening to the lyrics, feeling like something bigger than myself had just occurred.

Promise me that you'll give faith a fighting chance . . .
And when you get the choice, to sit it out or dance . . . I hope you dance.

I hadn't sat it out, I'd danced. I hadn't known the steps. I'd tripped and fallen and made a mess of it—a horrible mess—but I'd danced. I'd tried and I'd failed, but I'd danced.

It was one of the worst nights of my life, if not *the* worst, yet it's the reason I learned to dance properly. And, as a result, I have rescued or found loving homes for over five hundred dogs.

CHAPTER FOUR

"Spycial" Charlie

On a beautiful, breezy morning in August, Sammy and I had taken a long walk in Riverside Park after her usual playtime and we were heading home. Across the grassy median, a man was walking his black German Shepherd/Akita mix.

"Hi, sweetheart," I called to the dog when he looked at Sammy and me. He seemed excited that I was talking to him and lunged forward in a playful way. "What a handsome boy you are!" He pulled against his leash trying to get to us, as his owner held him back. "He's gorgeous," I said. "How old is he?" To this day, I'm not sure what made me cross the median and approach them.

"He's almost a year old. I have to find him a home. My wife won't let me keep him anymore."

"Oh, how sad. Why not?" I asked.

The man shrugged his hunched shoulders. He had greasy black hair and was extremely thin. I looked down at the dog. "What's his name?" I inquired.

"Spice."

Spice? I thought. *What an odd name.* But the man was a bit odd as well, so it was not that surprising. "Where did you get him?" By now Sammy and Spice were sniffing each other and starting the play dance.

"From the shelter, when he was a puppy," the man mumbled. "My wife keeps him in a crate all day, and I walk him once a day."

My mouth hung open. Besides Sammy's history, this was my first toe dip into animal cruelty and neglect. "In a crate, why?" He shrugged his hunched shoulders, yet again. "Well, maybe I can help," I offered.

I had met a woman at the park who rescued dogs. I was amazed and impressed when I heard that she spent her money helping animals that were not her own. If she could help so many, then why couldn't I help this one? Now that I thought I "knew" dogs and what they needed, what they thought and felt, the idea of this one living in a crate broke my heart. What if it were my Princess? "Well, I have to help him," I said to the man. "Of course, I'll help him."

The month before, Jude and I had hired a lawyer to launch a legal fight against our landlord who was trying to evict us because we had Sammy, even though there were many dogs in the building. Unfortunately, the law in New York states the landlord can decide who can have a dog and who cannot. We lived on the Upper West Side in a great, old apartment building on the twenty-third floor with fantastic views. Since our landlord wanted our apartment so that he could raise the rent, he gave us an ultimatum: get rid of the dog or leave. We fought him, and at the last minute he backed down, asking for money instead. Because of this, we could not adopt another dog.

The next day, my friend, actress and animal lover, Susan (Suze) Misner and I showed up at Spice's apartment. My plan was to take him to the dog park to see if anyone I knew would adopt him. I had asked Suze to accompany me to their apartment, as I didn't want to go alone, knowing how odd the man was. I rang the bell outside the building and was buzzed in. We could not have prepared for what we were about to encounter.

"Second floor," I heard a friendly female voice say.

When we arrived on the second floor, we were met by a small woman who looked to be in her mid-forties, with brown hair put up in a bun, wearing a t-shirt and jeans.

"Hi, come on in. Which one of you is Sylva?" she asked.

I walked toward her outstretched hand. "I am. Hi, how are—" I stopped mid-sentence. I could not believe what I was looking at through the open door. This was long before any hoarding shows were on TV. As I entered, I gasped! Filthy clothes, garbage, and newspapers covered every inch of the floor. Massive mounds of stuff climbed to the ceiling, all around the room. In the middle of what was supposed to be the living room was a dirty crate. Inside sat Spice. To them, he was just more stuff.

There was a stench in the apartment, a mixture of moldy, rotting food, dog feces, and body odor. I felt so nauseated I could barely talk. The thought of these people and this dog living in such squalor made me sick. I looked at poor Spice in the crate and thought, *What the hell, lady!* I didn't ask her name or introduce Suze.

At that moment, their seven-year-old son, who had been standing in what was once the kitchen, caught my attention. He smiled at me with sad eyes. "Hi," I said, smiling back, caught off guard.

"Hi," he responded.

My god, this poor boy has to live here too!

Their residence was actually two apartments that had been merged together. The woman's father had owned the building, and she had inherited the property. Mind you, this was fabulous, prime real estate, one block away from Riverside Drive on New York's Upper West Side.

"Where is Spice's leash?" I asked. I wanted to get us out of there immediately. My dear friend stood at the front door with her mouth agape.

Just then the husband walked into the room and pointed to the floor where Suze was standing. "There it is," he said, as he leaned down to pick it up amongst the used Chinese food containers. "Thanks for taking him."

"I'll do what I can, but if I don't find him a home today I'll have to bring him back and try again tomorrow." The thought of that made me cringe.

I was amazed neither of them mentioned or apologized for the squalor they lived in, as if it was normal. Then the father thanked me, and I thought I caught a fleeting glimpse of shame in his eyes.

"Would you two like some coffee, before you go?" the mother asked.

Coffee! Are you kidding me, lady? "No, no thank you," I politely said, as Suze violently shook her head back and forth. Then I noticed something move behind the woman. It looked like a white mass. "Oh my god," I gasped, leaning down to pick up the little white moving object coming toward me. "Oh my god!"

"Yes, she needs a haircut," the wife said.

She needs more than a haircut, lady! I wanted to scream and shake her.

"Oh my god," I heard Suze say.

The little white ball of a dog was now covering me with kisses. Sugar was her name, and she was a makeover waiting to happen. Her hair was matted so tight that she must have been in pain. Hard and crusty poop covered her bottom. I took a deep breath and told myself to concentrate on one dog at a time. Spice had started crying to get out of his crate, so I reached over to let him out.

"Thanks again." The man did his best to smile at me as he leashed him up.

I put Sugar on the couch that was covered in clothes and old newspapers. "Okay, fingers crossed," I said, as Spice, Suze, and I headed out the door.

We couldn't get to the dog park fast enough. We wanted to tell anyone who was interested in Spice about his dreadful living situation, so someone would take pity on him and adopt the Shepherd/Akita mix immediately. For two hours, he ran and played and had the time of his life. He was great with the other dogs and all the people, but no one there that day was willing to adopt him. When it was time to go home, at least Spice was exhausted. I knew he would sleep well.

I said goodbye to Suze, who had to get home to New Jersey, and Spice and I headed back toward his apartment. I racked my brain trying to think who might want him yet, by the time I had reached his front door, no one had come to mind. "I'm sorry, Spice," I said, as we came up to his building. "I promise I'll get you out of here, soon."

And then something happened that broke my heart. Spice lay down, put his head on my foot, and let out a cry—a real wail from deep in his belly. He was begging me not to take him back in there. I sat down on the walkway with him and ran my hand down his beautiful thick black coat.

"I don't know what to do Spice. I can't take you home with me," I said as he looked up with pleading eyes. Then I realized it was Friday evening, and my landlord would not be in the building until Monday. If I brought him back to our apartment, that would give me two days to find him a home. "Come on, boy, we're out of here."

Spice couldn't believe it. He kept glancing at me and nudging my leg on the way uptown, as if to ask, "Is this for real?" When we walked in the door, Sammy remembered the dog from the park and welcomed him immediately. Jude came home a few hours later.

"Sylva, we can't keep him."

"I know. It's just for the weekend. We have to find him a home by Monday."

"Okay, I'll call everyone I know tomorrow. 'Spice' is a stupid name," my husband added. "How about 'Spycial,' because he's special?"

"You got it honey. That's very creative."

The next day, Jude's brother put me in touch with his friend, who had had two Boxers, one of whom had recently passed away. "I really want another Boxer. I'm not much of a Shepherd person," he told me.

"But this dog is very special. If you met him, you would really love him," I pleaded. I also mentioned that he would be going back to live in a crate, prodding my brother-in-law's friend to at least make an effort to see if they might be a match.

Later that day, Spycial and I walked uptown to meet the guy and his white, deaf Boxer in Riverside Park. The dogs immediately got along. The guy agreed to try it overnight, so I walked with them to his apartment, where I met his wife and seventeen-year-old son, who seemed very nice. An hour later, when I closed the door behind me, I began to cry. I knew they would keep him, and I was so grateful that this dog would now have a good life.

The next day I showed up at Spice's old apartment and told them about his new home. The odd couple seemed indifferent about the good news. I offered to take Sugar, their little, white dog with the matted fur, to a groomer, which they allowed. When we returned, I tried everything I could to have them relinquish her to me, so that I could find her a new home, but the wife refused to give her up. *Well, at least Sugar is more comfortable with the fur mats removed, which is better than nothing*, I assured myself. But I had hoped the lady would allow me to take her out of that garbage pile for good.

A few months later, I got a call from the woman telling me social services was threatening to take her son away. She cried and begged me to help. I spent two days cleaning out one of her rooms, making it into a lovely bedroom for her son. However, my efforts ended up being a temporary Band-Aid. A few years later, the boy was removed because of the unsafe living conditions. Eventually, the husband gained custody after the couple divorced. The hoarding had been her problem, not his. I heard from a neighbor that after the son left, the mother started grooming Sugar regularly and taking her out for walks.

A year after I rescued Spycial, now renamed Charlie by his new owner, Jude and I decided to move to Los Angeles. I called the guy to ask him if he was sure he wanted to keep Charlie. I had hoped to bring him with us to LA, but my brother-in-law's friend assured me Charlie was in his forever home.

"Okay, but if you ever change your mind, let me know," I said before I hung up.

As I prepared to move to LA, I remember thinking I might never see Spycial Charlie again.

Boy, was I wrong.

Chapter Five

Flying to "La La" Land

The thought of putting Sammy on a plane terrified me. She was now 45-pounds. Too big to fly under my seat. She would have to go into the cargo hold, along with the luggage.

"Maybe I should drive out," I suggested to Jude one evening while we were on the phone. My husband had gone back to work in LA. It was up to me to pack us up and get the hell out of town. 9/11 had happened three months before. The city and our lives had been changed forever.

"We don't have a car," he reminded me. "You can't drive. We sold it, remember?"

"I know, but I can rent one." I was trying to figure out a way to get Sammy to LA without terrifying her with a five-hour flight and, in the process, prevent me from having a heart attack. I would have been happy to stay put, but between the terrorist attack and now having enough acting credits to open doors for me in LA, it was time to head back west.

New York was like a war zone, with flyers of lost loved ones posted up and down Lexington Avenue and people working around the clock where the towers once were, clearing the debris. Ironically, a few weeks after the disaster, I began rehearsing a play at the Tribeca Playhouse downtown. In it, I played a German movie star after World War II. It was surreal because I had to walk from the subway with a mask on, so as not to breathe the fumes from the site, and into a play about the aftermath of war.

I had known two people whose lives were taken on 9/11. One of them was a gal from the park, who lived alone with her dog and had been in the restaurant at the top of Tower 1 for a seminar that morning. I always wonder if she was one of the people who jumped. Her parents took her companion back to Connecticut to live with them, and a lovely plaque was placed in the dog park with her name on it. The other was a charming fireman who had worked with me on the movie *Spiderman*. Spiderman saved my baby from my burning apartment in the film, so they had real firemen working with us. One of them, Tom Foley, hung out with me all day. Though he loved being a firemen, he confessed that he wanted to be an actor. *People* magazine had named him one of the most eligible bachelors of the year because he was very handsome, as all New York firemen seem to be. My jaw hit the floor when I saw a picture of him on the news one night after the hijacked planes brought the Towers down. Devastating.

"I have an idea," I said to Jude the next day, when driving didn't seem like the best option. "I'm going to buy a crate now, a month before we leave. Then, I'm going to put your sound machine on top of the crate to generate white noise, so it mimics the sound of a plane engine. I'm going to keep her in there for a few minutes a day, then gradually build up to five hours over the course of the month."

Jude was impressed. "That could work."

The first time I had to gently coax Sammy into the crate with treats. It took a while, as the crate reminded her of her time at the vet's office and she wanted nothing to do with it. After I locked her in, she whimpered and stared at me from behind the bars as if to say, "Why are you doing this?" But, by the end of the week, she seemed to like her crate. She curled up on the soft blankets I put in there, along with "Elyphant," her favorite stuffed elephant toy.

When we left our apartment for Kennedy Airport that cold January morning a month later, my Princess was an expert flyer, even though she had never left the ground. I knew Sammy would feel comfortable in her crate, but I now had other fears. Would the airline workers forget to put her on the plane? Would we be hijacked and taken down? Would they forget to unload her, if they remembered to put her on the plane? Would she be stolen when we landed, before I could get to her? I was a bundle of nerves as I went through security to the boarding gate.

Oh, this is great! I thought as I approached the waiting area. The windows looked out onto the tarmac, where I could see the luggage being loaded. *Thank God*, I thought as I glued myself to the window and watched the men driving the piled bags toward the plane. They told me she would be boarded last, so I did not panic when I didn't see her right away. But then, a police car came driving toward the plane with sirens blaring. My mind jumped to where everyone's did at that time when we heard sirens—*terrorists!*

Suddenly, out of nowhere, came a black sedan. It pulled up behind the police car and out stepped George Pataki, then governor of New York. It actually made me laugh out loud. At least, I thought, my fear of being hijacked was a longshot. Our plane would now be crawling with security.

And then I saw her, my little Princess, peering out of the bars of her crate as the luggage car rounded the bend. "There she is!" I said to a woman standing next to me. "There's my girl." I remember getting teary eyed, feeling how confused she must be. But as I watched them load her onto the plane, I breathed a sigh of relief. If we were going down, we were going down together.

"Don't worry. She'll be fine," the woman assured me.

I decided to do my best to relax, which would give me five hours of peace before we landed. But all through the flight I imagined Sammy down in the dark. *Uh!* I thought. In my preparations of getting her used to the crate, I had not put her in a dark room. *She must be terrified. Either that, or she's having a great sleep,* I assured myself.

Once we landed, I rushed off the plane to greet my husband, who was waiting at the gate for me. "Hurry," I said. "We have to drive to another area of the airport to pick her up."

"Well, hello to you too, my Princess, and welcome to LA," he said before registering what I had just told him.

Jude had started calling me "my Princess" soon after we began dating. On our honeymoon, my husband expanded my nickname to "The Dolphin Princess," because of my swimming ability. I loved the name "The Dolphin Princess" and eventually wrote a children's book with that title. Coincidentally, I called Sammy my Princess, as well, so there were a few princesses in the family.

"We have to go all the way across the airport to pick her up?" Jude asked. There was panic in his voice. "Someone could steal her before we get there!"

"My thought, exactly. So let's hurry!" Usually my husband drove like an old man, but that day he was on a mission to rescue his princess before she could be sold into canine slavery, and he was her knight in speeding metal car armor. "There she is! There she is! Princess Girl! We're here, my Princess!" Sammy had spotted us and was beating her tail so hard against the inside of the carrier that we could hear it from across the hanger. "We're here, Beauty Princess," I said again as I let our girl out and immediately leashed her. Next I reached inside the carrier for the ceramic dog angel I had taped to the roof to watch over her during her flight. Jude had gotten it in a gift shop in Solvang, California. It was a small Shepherd head with wings. "Mama and Daddy are here," I said, as I gave her a big hug and kiss.

The workers standing around the loading dock had seen, I'm sure, a lot of happy greetings by people to their traveling pets. Yet I don't think they had ever heard anyone like me. A few laughed and smiled, while the others glared like I was a psycho. I could hear them talking as I left: "Man, that lady needs to have a kid. Why does she love her *dog* so much?"

But I didn't care. Sammy and I were safe in LA. "Thanks and have a great day!" I smiled and waved to them. Then the three of us were on our way to start our new lives.

CHAPTER SIX

Daddy's Girl and My Handsome

Jude and I had not yet lived together 24/7. Before we were married we had separate residences, but mostly stayed at mine on West 57th Street. Shortly after our wedding, I had moved into his West End Avenue apartment, and he had gone off to Los Angeles for work.

I always said that if I ever moved back to LA, I would like to live near the equestrian center in Burbank. I'd spent time around the area before I moved back to New York, and I loved the small town feel of it and the fact that there were horses everywhere. Seeing that we were in a competitive, crazy business, I thought it would be a nice balance to live over the hill from Hollywood and feel like we were in a different world.

Before I arrived in LA, Jude found a three-story town house which overlooked the horse trails in front of the equestrian center. I got to work upgrading and decorating our new place the moment we moved in, which was something I had always wanted to do, if I ever owned my own house. I am very passionate about home improvement. If I wasn't an actress, I would probably have been a full-time interior decorator. So I loved every minute of it.

It was an exciting time in my life. I had a new husband, a new dog, a new home, and I was embarking on a new career in LA. No longer was I the lonely, struggling actress I had been the last time I lived here.

"I think I met a sister for Sammy," Jude announced, a few weeks after we had moved into the town house. "She's the same color and looks like a smaller version of her."

That was hard to believe, because my Princess was the most unique, gorgeous strawberry blonde color. A real strawberry blonde—unlike her mother, me, who got it out of a bottle.

"She was at the park chasing squirrels and Sammy seemed to like her. The foster woman said she could bring her over tomorrow. The dog's name is Mazie. She's almost a year old."

My husband had such excitement in his voice, I figured why not.

"Hi, Mazie," Jude said with a smile on his face, while reaching down to pet the 32-pound Shiba Inu/Cattle Dog as she walked in our door the next day. A group called Bill Foundation had rescued her from the high-kill South Central shelter.

My Princess was very excited to have another dog in the house and immediately picked up her white stuffed toy and put it in her potential sister's mouth, while still holding onto it. Mazie had obviously played tug of war before, and the game was intense and competitive, yet playful. They were a good match. Then Mazie darted around the room like a bullet, while Sammy tried to keep up.

This new little canine's ears crinkled and looked like a fortune cookie when she was happy, and she had the most beautiful gold-and-black eyes that resembled marbles. She also had the longest whiskers on a dog I had ever seen, almost like a mouse's. She was an adorable, sweet, unique creature.

"You can do a week trial if you want," her foster mom, Tessa, said. "That's the policy of Bill Foundation."

"I don't think that's necessary, do you?" I asked Jude.

"No, not really. She's great and Sammy loves her."

I turned back to Tessa. "Yeah, we'll adopt her. What do we have to do?"

The next morning Sammy sat and stared at me. She had spent the previous evening playing with Mazie, but now she wanted nothing to do with this puppy that was overstaying her welcome. She looked at me and then to the little dog, as if to say, "Why is she still here?"

"Mazie's your new sister," I explained to Sammy. "She's not leaving. She's staying." My Princess cocked her head back and forth as she always did when I spoke to her. To this day, she is the most intelligent, inquisitive dog I have ever met. She always wanted to know every move I made and why I was making it. I had spent the last year and a half talking to her as though she were a human, and because of this, her mind was very sharp. She seemed to understand everything I said.

"Mazie's staying." I repeated. "Now go play with her."

But from then on, Sammy hardly ever played with her sister again. It was the strangest thing, as if she decided she was too grown up for such frivolous interaction. Or perhaps she was trying to tell me she would have preferred to be an only dog after all and not have to share her parents with anyone. She had always been the belle of the dog park in New York, so this sudden change saddened me.

Regardless, a few days later, Noreen, the rescue group volunteer, was sitting in our kitchen finalizing the adoption for Mazie. As she fretted over every detail of the contract with me, I remember judging her to be incredibly anal.

"I notice you don't have a collar and tag on your dog," she commented in a critical voice.

"Well, I take it off when we're in the house," I said. "I've always done that."

"That's a mistake. Anything can happen at any time, anywhere, and now you live in earthquake country. What if the doors fly open and she gets scared and bolts?" She looked at me and raised her eyebrow.

"I never thought of that, but you're right," I agreed. The idea of Sammy getting lost again terrified me. Even though she was microchipped, why should I expect someone to go out of their way to have her scanned when they could just call me immediately? I had Sammy's collar and tags back on before Noreen had time to lower her eyebrow. They remained on her after that and only came off while she was having a bath, with one last exception—the day she died. We imposed the same rule for Mazie, soon to be referred to as "Daddy's girl."

We were settling into Los Angeles beautifully. Jude was playing Mike Novik on the beloved TV series *24* while I was working consistently, guest starring on one-hour dramas like *Cold Case*, *Bones*, *Without a Trace*, and *Prison Break*. Plus, I was doing small parts in big movies. We had held off trying to get pregnant because I wanted to get my career rolling. Now that it was, we decided to start trying.

I had gone through one round of in vitro fertilization (IVF) and was gearing up for a second. I had sworn I would never do IVF, yet there I was, sticking needles into my belly. If round two didn't work, our fertility doctor suggested using an egg donor. I didn't want an egg donor, but I would have adopted if Jude had been open to it.

"If this doesn't work, I want to adopt a baby from Africa," I proclaimed to him one day. I had always felt a bond with Africa, though to this day I have never been there. When I was twenty-four, I committed to help financially support an African child by mail. Soon I was supporting three children in need, one from Ethiopia, one from West Ghana, and one from India. I was thrilled when, years later, it became popular to adopt from Africa so more kids could be helped. "You know," I added "if I ever go to Africa, I'm either not coming back, or I'm coming back with a baby."

My husband rubbed his bald head, then ran his fingers along his chin and rolled his eyes. In his humorous way he said, "Then don't come back. The only way I'll have a kid is if it's our own."

The thought of sticking more needles in my stomach was not very appetizing, and it was very expensive. To a friend urging me to try a third time if round two failed (she had gotten pregnant in round three), I informed her, "I am willing to try a second time. But that's it. If it doesn't work, I'm not doing it again."

While we were at dinner one night, the wife of one of Jude's friends told me that there was an unfinished furniture store on Magnolia Blvd. "It's right up your alley, Sylva. You can finish and paint the pieces yourself."

I went there the following day, bought a few nightstands for our bedroom and decided to stain them green. "Come on, damn it!" I exclaimed out loud when I realized the last bit of stain in the can would not be enough to finish the side of the second nightstand. "Shit!" I hated when that happened.

"Shit!" I said again, when there was no parking space in front of the furniture store and nowhere on Magnolia Blvd either. The first time I had been there, I had noticed an open gate on the side of the building leading to the back of the store. *I guess I can park back there*, I thought. I drove down the alley, parked, quickly got out, and headed toward the back door.

"Ruff! Ruff! Ruff!" I heard behind me, as I reached for the door. There were four other people in the driveway, three customers, and one of the owners, who I had met the day before.

"Ruff, Ruff!"

As I turned around, I felt a hand push the back of my shoulder and nudge me toward the sound. It was a gentle, definite push, but when I looked over my shoulder, there was no one there. *That's weird*, I thought. I then saw the dog. A 27-pound, brown and black Terrier mix with big, soulful, brown eyes, chained to a doghouse in the back of the parking lot. He was staring at me.

"Don't mind him," the owner, a round, bald-headed man said.

I walked up to the Terrier. "Hi, little guy. How are you?" The dog pushed into my arms and nuzzled against my chest, wagging his tail as if his battery had just been turned on. I looked at the dirty doghouse and the chain around his neck. "Why is he chained up?" I asked.

"We let him loose at night when we lock the gate."

"Why does he live back here?" I couldn't understand why this adorable dog was kept in this sort of living condition.

"He was my mother's dog, but she died three years ago," he explained as he waved to the customers, who had by now gotten in their cars and were driving away.

"We had him at our house in the backyard, but we moved him here last year," a voice behind me said. I turned to see a dark-haired woman in her forties coming out of the store. She carried the smell of pine on her clothing, pungent from the furniture she and her husband sold.

"That's my wife," the owner told me.

"Hi. So why can't you keep him *in* your house?" I inquired.

"I'm allergic to dogs, so he lived in our backyard. But we thought he would do better here," she explained.

I looked down at the proud boy who had by now glued himself to my leg. I couldn't imagine what it must have been like for him, living alone in a backyard. I didn't believe her claim that she was allergic to this Terrier, especially if she was not allergic to all the smells of wood and paint she worked around every day. "I'll take him," I said. "I'll take him and find him a home. He shouldn't have to live like this."

"You won't put him to sleep, will you?" she asked in a seemingly sympathetic voice.

"I would never put a dog to sleep, unless they were suffering. I want to find him a proper home," I informed her. She turned and walked back into the store without saying goodbye to the dog.

"That would be great. I know my mom would like that. I promised her we would take care of him, but this was the best I could do," the man said.

"Don't worry about it," I assured him.

While I put the dog in my car, the owner went into his store. When he came out, he was carrying a can of green stain and some papers. "No charge for the stain," he said. "Here are the shot records, and the microchip info you should have."

"What's his name, and how old is he?" I asked as I got in the car. The dog was smiling and banging his tail on the seat beside me.

"Bo Bo. He's about nine. My mother got him out of the shelter when he was three, she had him for three years, and we had him for three years. So, yeah, nine."

"He's going to have a good life now. I'll let you know what happens." As I pulled away, Bo Bo never looked back.

I called Jude on the way home. "Hi, honey, don't freak out, but I'm coming home with a dog. I got him at the furniture store. I think his old owner sent me there to get him, because I felt her push me toward him when he barked." I knew Jude was not thrilled about my phone call, and he probably thought I made up the part about being pushed by the dead owner, but he, and Sammy, and Mazie were at the door to greet us when we got home. I knew nothing about introducing dogs properly at that time, so I just walked Bo Bo into the house, hoping for the best. We were lucky, because everyone accepted each other immediately. I later learned that the proper way to introduce dogs is on neutral territory, outside, and on leash.

"He stinks," Jude said. "He needs a bath. Wait a minute, *where* did you get this dog?"

"At the furniture store."

Jude's eyes widened. "I think I saw him last week, running down the street when I went to the theater. The theater people said he roamed the neighborhood at night all the time."

"Well, that would make sense, since the theater is across the street from the store where he lived and the guy said they let him loose at night. But he would have had to get under the fence and cross that busy street to get there." The thought made my stomach tighten. This dog was the sweetest, proudest, dearest animal I had ever met.

"Wow. That's amazing," Jude said to Bo Bo. "I just saw you last week!"

"Too bad you didn't try to get him then." I looked at my husband with my mouth agape. I couldn't imagine seeing a dog wandering down the street without trying to help. "Thank God he didn't get hit by a car," I added.

"I was about to see a play," Jude said. "But he's here now, so that's all that matters, and remember the dog I did rescue in New York?" Jude had saved a dog after the Riverside stray incident: a huge, sweet, mangy bulldog, wandering the park with a chain around his neck. My rescue friend Marilyn had taken him and found him a great home in Soho.

The next day I made flyers for Beau Bo—Jude's new spelling of his name—and put an ad in a free newspaper, advertising the Terrier needed a home. I had no intention of keeping him. I was trying to get pregnant and I did not want three dogs. Two was enough.

I got a call that night. "Hi. I saw your ad in the paper about the Terrier," an older woman with a sweet voice explained. "I just want to warn you that you need to do a home check, and charge a fee for the dog. There are bad people out there who will take free dogs, only to sell them to research facilities, abuse them, or sell them for bait in dog fights."

"Wow, really!"

"Yes, really. So please, make sure you put him in a good home."

I wasn't planning on giving Beau Bo to just anyone, but I had not thought about charging a fee. I was now aware of the things that people could do when they took free dogs.

"Well, thank you for the advice and information. I'll be careful."

A few days later, I drove Beau Bo to Glendale to meet a lovely retired woman who had seen my ad. She had a nice house with a safe yard and promised to walk him every day. She was also very affectionate toward the nine-year-old Terrier.

"Please be careful he doesn't get out," I said about five times before I left. "He will bolt if the door opens." I knew this because, the night I brought him home, I was walking him with the leash attached to his collar, and it slipped over his head, and he ran. When he stopped to smell something, I dived on top of him. That would be the last time I ever walked a dog on a collar. The next day, I had bought Beau Bo a soft nylon choke collar that I attached to a leash, and used only to walk him. The collar with his tags stayed on at all times.

"Let's do a one-week trial," I said to the retired lady. "If it works out, you can pay me an adoption fee of $100."

Beau Bo was up on the couch looking out the window as I drove away. *He's in good hands,* I thought. *I don't have to worry, he will be very loved and spoiled.*

The next morning my phone rang.

"Hi, Sylva. I just want you to know that Beau Bo got out last night when my husband left the gate open. He came back about an hour later but then, this morning, he got out again when my husband opened the gate to get his car out."

"Where is he now?" I screamed into the phone.

"Well, he came back again, but my husband thinks he's ugly, so I don't know—"

"I'll be there in ten minutes!"

Beau Bo was in the same spot, looking out the window, when I pulled up. I could see him smile with excitement when he saw me. Then he ran toward the front door. "Come on, Beaubs, we're out of here," I said after she had closed the door behind us.

When we got home, Jude was as furious as I was. "How can anyone call him ugly? What an asshole! And to let him get out twice? What's wrong with these people?"

"I think he was trying to get back to me, but then he realized the only way to do that was to go back to their house." Beau Bo had claimed me for himself the day after I rescued him, but I couldn't keep him. "I'm going to take him to another woman who called me. She has a six-year-old son, and they want a smallish dog."

Jude looked at me sideways. "We should just keep him. He's happy here."

"I don't want three dogs and a baby. It will be too hard in this town house for me to walk them. Say goodbye. I think the other home is going to work out."

The minute I pulled up in front of the new woman's house, I got a bad feeling. She lived on a very busy street in a not-so-nice neighborhood. Beau Bo and I got out of the car, and I rang the bell. I heard barking from the backyard.

"Oh, he's adorable. Isn't he adorable?" the lady said to her son when she opened the door.

"Oh, I love him. He's so sweet," the son squealed.

"Do you have other dogs?" I asked. "I heard dogs barking."

"Yes, we have two big, outdoor dogs that live in the backyard, but they are very sweet." She ushered us into her house and walked toward the kitchen window.

Funny, I thought, *she didn't mention any other dogs on the phone.*

"See, there they are?" she said as she pointed out the window. "But Beau Bo will live in the house with us." Before I could respond, one of her dogs pushed open the back kitchen door and went straight for my Terrier. Her dog was not happy to have a strange canine in his house, especially if *he* couldn't live in it. I immediately jumped in and grabbed Beau Bo, before anything could happen.

Once the woman got her dog outside, she assured me that that would never happen again and that they would take Beau Bo in the front to do his business.

"He'll be out the front door the minute it opens and get hit by a car, if your dog doesn't get to him first," I explained to her. "Why don't you just let your dogs live *in* the house? They'll be a lot happier and then you don't have to worry about them hurting a little dog."

The thought made her wince and her son started crying. "Sorry, but it's not going to work. Come on, Beaubs," I whispered, "We're out of here."

"Why can't we keep Beau Bo? Why?" I heard her son wail, as I closed the door behind us.

I was sitting at the kitchen table watching horses walk by on the path behind our house, mulling over the day. Sammy and Mazie were staring at me, willing me to look at the clock and see that it was five minutes to their dinnertime.

"Let's just keep him," Jude said as he came in the door. "We'll figure out how to walk them if we have a baby. He has a good home here, he's old, and probably won't be around much longer anyway. He's totally housebroken, doesn't bark, and is good with the dogs. He's not a problem, so let's keep him."

Jude was right. Beau Bo was the perfect dog, and he did not bark. I had not heard him bark since he got my attention that first day, which I thought was weird. Beau Bo was not a barker, yet he had known who to bark at to get off that chain.

"You're right. He probably won't live that much longer, anyway," I said. "And I do love him."

The next day I got Beau Bo his official name tag and had him licensed as our third dog.

Me and my grandmother's animals

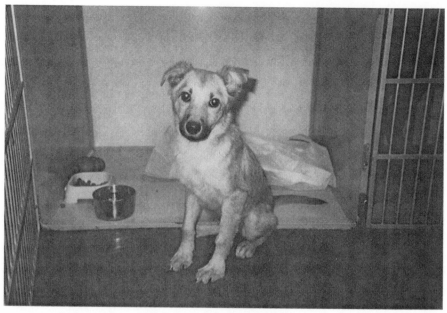

Sammy as a puppy at the vet

Sammy's inquisitive head tilt

Sammy & BFF Lucy

My Beauty Princess in East Hampton

"Spycial" Charlie

Mazie aka Daddy's Girl

Beau Bo aka my Handsome

CHAPTER SEVEN

If I Only Knew

I had started to think about doing volunteer work with a rescue group I read about in *The Pet Press*. The founder of the group was an actress as well. After reading about them, it felt like the right place for me to extend myself, perhaps by volunteering my time at weekend pet adoptions. I put the paper aside with the thought of calling them, as soon as I knew if we were going to have a baby.

The answer came quickly. Evidently, it was not that easy for me to get pregnant; round two of IVF did not work, either.

"That's it. We tried," I told my husband, after sobbing for about an hour.

"Are you sure you don't want to try one more time?" Jude felt terrible.

"No. It's not meant to be. Let's leave it alone."

I was forty by then, and he was fifty-five. The odds of us having a healthy baby were not great.

It's amazing to me, as I look back now, how fast I moved on emotionally from wanting to have a baby to accepting that I couldn't get pregnant. I love kids and I think, at that point, I would have been a great mom, yet intuitively, I knew that my life was going to be about something else. If Jude had agreed to adopt, I would have, but my husband was fifteen years older than I and working constantly on television and in movies such as *The Manchurian Candidate* with Meryl Streep and *High Crimes* with Ashley Judd. He was also a singer and producing his fourth album and putting his '50s-'60s band together. He did not want to adopt a child. "If we have our own I could deal with it, but if we adopt a kid and there are problems, it's going to do me in," he said, urging me to understand.

I understood.

Now that I knew I would have a lot of time on my hands when I wasn't working, I called the animal rescue group I had read about to look into volunteering. "We have adoptions every Sunday at the PetSmart," the woman said. "You're welcome to come this weekend if you like. We always need help."

That Sunday morning I got up early to walk our three dogs before heading to the adoption event. I had no idea what to expect as I entered the PetSmart, located in the Central San Fernando Valley, a forty-minute drive from our house in Burbank. "Hi, I'm here to volunteer," I said to the stressed-out young blonde woman in charge. She was setting up the dog crates while ordering other volunteers to fill up water bowls.

"Great, just hold onto that dog," she said, pointing to a rather large Shepherd/Golden Retriever mix that had walked through the door. "His foster mom can't stay."

"Hi," the foster mom said, as she handed me the leash. "I'll be back at two p.m. to get him. Thanks." She was out the door as quickly as she had come in.

The Shepherd mix looked at me as if to say, "And who are *you*?"

"Hi, big guy, what's your name?" I responded to his inquisitive stare.

"That's Lucky," a teenage volunteer informed me. "He was given up by his owner who kept him in the backyard his whole life, but now he's with a great foster. He's going to get a wonderful home." The boy smiled wide, his eyes shining with intelligence and concern. "He's one of my favorites."

Lucky was still staring up at me as I bent down to pet his head. "I can't believe people make their dogs live outside. I don't see the point of that."

"Get used to it," the blonde volunteer in charge barked at me. "Most people are idiots and don't realize how to properly treat their dogs. You have to learn to hold your tongue around here and interview them without giving anything away. We only place dogs as indoor pets. They're more social than people and need to be with their pack. So we ask people to fill out an application first, then we talk to them. Makes them answer the questions more honestly if they can't read into our intentions."

"We do home checks too," the teenager added proudly.

"*If* their application is good," the blonde corrected him. "So just watch and learn today. You'll get the hang of it. If you want, you can walk the dogs too. They need to get out of their crates every hour."

She was so serious, I wondered if she had always been like that or if dealing with the public and animal neglect had made her that way.

Taking the leash out of my hand, she gently nudged Lucky into one of the large, readied crates. Within the next few minutes, eight more dogs and three more volunteers arrived, and the canines were placed in the appropriate size crates.

"We get them from all over," I heard the boy telling a prospective adopter. "This one," he said, pointing to a Poodle mix that had a fresh haircut, "is from the South Central Shelter. He was going to be put to sleep because he was in such bad shape. You couldn't even see he was a dog behind all his hair. A lot of the dogs there have been neglected and abused, but so have a lot of dogs from the other shelters in LA as well. And they all kill dogs." The boy shook his head in a way that let those of us listening know he was now privy to the dark side of this life. I had yet to learn it, but as the day went on, I was starting to get a glimpse. Every dog there was the victim of a neglectful or abusive situation from all over town. From all walks of life.

Some of the dogs that came for adoption that day in hopes of getting a new, loving, forever home were: a Dachshund mix who was found wandering the streets in Van Nuys, emaciated with mange; a sweet golden-colored crop-eared Pitbull who had been chained up most of her five years in Hollywood; a six-month-old Cattle Dog from North Hollywood who had been left in a backyard when the owners moved; and a senior Chihuahua who had been bred so many times her teats were the largest I had ever seen. A Ridgeback mix who had been starved by some people in Beverly Hills before he was rescued was there as well.

"This is only a taste of it," the wise boy said. "There are millions more on the streets, in backyards, homes, and shelters everywhere. More than you can imagine."

Did he take a college course on the world of animal abuse? I wondered.

"Why are you giving her up?" the blonde asked a couple and their child who had brought their dog over to us a few moments later. The animal was a small, dainty, very thin, gray-and-white Greyhound, mixed with Shepherd, and God only knew what else. She weighed around 25-pounds.

"I don't think we have the time for her," the father said.

But before he could finish his sentence, his daughter, who was about five-years-old, chimed in, "He keeps her in the garage." The father froze and gave a weak smile to cover his feelings. He then said something to his daughter in Armenian.

Though *my* father was Armenian, I never did learn the language. But I could tell he wanted to shut her up before she could say anything else. *Out of the mouths of babes,* I thought.

"We'll take her, and I'll pay for her boarding," an older volunteer interrupted. She told me later that she wanted to get the dog away from them before he changed his mind out of embarrassment.

Wow, I thought. *She's like that woman in New York who pays to rescue dogs herself.* I was very impressed.

The mother handed over the dog's leash, and the family walked away, their tails between their legs. To think that this adorable, sweet, little animal had been imprisoned in a garage blew my mind.

As the day progressed, I wondered what I was doing there. Did I really want to spend my time sitting in a pet store witnessing firsthand the underbelly of life? Shouldn't I be at a movie or having lunch with a friend or, even better, curled up with a good book at home with my husband and my own dogs?

The answer was, "No." I felt compelled to stay and spent the rest of the day holding Trixie's leash. We renamed her after hearing the family call her an Armenian name I had never heard of. Trixie spent most of the day staring into my eyes as I petted and assured the loving dog that her life was about to get a lot better. I wondered what Jude would say if I brought her home. I felt myself bonding with the little mix of a girl, but I couldn't bring another animal home.

Trixie had obviously been ignored. She was enjoying being the center of everyone's affection, and I was falling in love. "I'll put her at cage-free doggy day care for the week," the older volunteer said, as if she could read my mind. "She'll be fine there."

As much as I wanted Trixie, it was a relief to know that she would be taken care of at the end of the day. I knew I would be back the next weekend—if for no other reason than to make sure the now rescued dog got the kind of home she deserved.

Miraculously, the following Sunday, a wonderful couple, Harry and Sarah, came to the pet store. They had recently adopted a dog named Shira, whose owner had been killed in a motorcycle accident. When they saw Trixie, they expressed interest in adopting her, too. So after the day's event ended, I went with the older volunteer to Harry and Sarah's for a home check.

Shira and Trixie bonded immediately. They ran in and out of the doggy door and chased one another around the quarter-acre yard. When they had worn themselves out, they collapsed together on one of the two dog beds in the living room of the house that they would now share. It was a great new beginning for Trixie, and ten years later, she is still with that lovely couple.

As the weeks went by, I continued to show up at eleven a.m. every Sunday for adoptions.

I discovered near my house a pet store called Pet Mania that took in only rescue animals, unlike other pet stores that sold only puppy mill puppies. These are puppies who come from parents raised in tiny crates, never see the light of day, and are bred over and over again. Astoundingly, this practice is legal in our country—a horrific fact for the animals that have to live in these appalling conditions.

At Pet Mania, I noticed that the dogs would be there week after week without getting adopted. "Hi," I said to Simone, the owner of the store at that time. "My name is Sylva. I would like to help these dogs get homes so that you can take more in. Would that be okay?" Simone had recently become a widow and had a young son. She pulled most of the dogs from high-kill shelters and saved their lives. She was from Germany, where dogs went everywhere with their people, and there was no overpopulation of animals roaming the streets. It's a different culture, and one we should learn from when it comes to how animals are treated.

Charlotte, a red-nosed Pitbull who was there that first day, had been left outside of the store for an employee to find in the morning. I made flyers with her picture and posted them at dog parks and at Runyon Canyon, a great hiking trail for people and dogs in Hollywood, where I had seen other dog flyers.

I got a call right away. "Hi, my name is Bill, and I'm calling about Charlotte, the Pitbull," the man said. "I saw her flyer at Runyon Canyon." After interviewing Bill, we decided to meet outside the Western Museum at Griffith Park. "I'll be in that area, and it's a good meeting place," he suggested.

I was thrilled for Charlotte. Bill was a single writer who worked from home and would spend all his time with her. *Please, God, let this work out and thank you for helping me put Charlotte in her forever, safe, loving, wonderful home,* I silently prayed.

"Hi, Charlotte," Bill called to her as she got out of my car. Charlotte was a very sweet, mellow, loving Pit who had showed no aggression toward people or other dogs. I felt their connection immediately as she dragged me toward her new daddy. "I *love* her!" Bill announced when he and Charlotte came back from their walk. I had stayed by the cars, watching them. "What do we do next?" he asked.

"I follow you home, if you're going there now, and I'll do the home check today, if that's okay?" I didn't want to take Charlotte back to a crate when she could sleep in a warm bed that night. I had him give me his driver's license. Then he took Charlotte in his car, as I drove behind them.

Bill's house turned out to be great for her, but after settling Charlotte into her new home, I told him two things. First, he would need to go to Pet Mania in the morning to pay an adoption fee and sign an adoption contract. Second, he should not let Charlotte hang out the window when he drove, as I noticed he had done when I followed him to his house. "She could jump out and get killed," I told him. I had never seen or heard of that happening, but common sense told me it easily could.

A week later, Bill called. "I wish I had listened to your advice."

"What happened?" I said with dread in my voice.

"Well, she'll be okay, but she jumped out the car window when she saw a squirrel, and a car hit her. Not hard, but hard enough to scare us both to death. Hard enough for me to never let that happen again."

"Well, thank God she didn't get killed!" I exclaimed. Why, I thought, did that even have to happen? I had told a seemingly smart man not to allow the opportunity for his Pitbull to jump out the window. It was amazing that I even had to tell him and yet, after being warned, he had allowed her to anyway. I was learning that finding wonderful homes for dogs was only part of the process. Once they were in those great homes, it was still not a guarantee of a safe life. Common sense was lacking in our culture, and it was about to take a toll on me.

Charlotte, however, lived another six fabulous years with Bill. He called me the day after she died of cancer to thank me for allowing him to adopt her.

At the time Charlotte got her new home, I was alternating weekends between showing Pet Mania dogs at the equestrian center on Saturdays and volunteering at adoptions on Sundays. The equestrian center had lots of people on the weekends for horse shows, and they had allowed me to set up an area to show dogs that needed homes. It was a great location, as most everyone there was an animal lover.

During the week, as time permitted, I would walk the dogs at the pet store and try to get them homes by posting flyers around town as well as the Internet. So I was spending a lot of time and energy helping dogs between my acting jobs. I found the balance refreshing, as my focus was not only on myself.

Then, lo and behold, Scarlett arrived at Pet Mania one day.

"What a cute Terrier!" I exclaimed when I saw the black-and-white, 45-pound, adorable-looking Disney dog. "Where did she come from?"

"Pulled from the shelter on her last day," one of the employees said.

"Oh my god, you're a cutie!" I loudly announced as I stroked her very skinny, wiry body. Scarlett was in a pen with another dog, a male Hound mix that had also been saved from the shelter.

"We have someone interested in him already, a great guy. He's coming back tonight with his wife," the employee informed me.

"You're a lucky boy," I said to the Hound dog. Then I turned to the employee, "If they want him, let me know so I can do the home check, okay?" I had told Simone I would help place the dogs only if I could do home checks. Home checks are very important because people will say anything to get a dog. I look to make sure that there are no holes in the fence, that the fence is high enough to prevent the dog from escaping, and that all gates have locks on them. Also, I make sure they will definitely be indoor dogs.

I once had a wealthy, seemingly intelligent man say his fences were seven feet tall. When we got to his house, he let the dog he wanted to adopt off leash in the backyard. That's when I noticed he had no fence around two sides of his property. A car on his busy street would have hit the dog within twenty-four hours. Needless to say, I didn't allow the adoption to go through.

"Scarlett is a nightmare on a leash when she sees other dogs." The employee wanted to make sure I understood, knowing my plan was to take her to the equestrian center.

How bad can she be? I thought, as I leashed her up with her nylon choke chain. "I'll take him too, just in case those people don't work out," I said, as I put a nylon choke and leash on the Hound as well. I had learned the hard way with Beau Bo to never walk a dog on a collar. Collars can slip over a dog's head, they can bolt, and be gone without their ID tag. "Come on, Andy and Ms. Scarlett, let's go try to find both of you a great home."

I had no idea what I was getting myself into.

The equestrian center was not only full of horses, but dogs as well. The minute we walked into the area where the arenas were, I realized I had made a huge mistake. I have never before or since met a dog like Scarlett. A Corgi, the first victim of her behavior, ran between his owner's legs and cried when he saw the Terrier lunging and screaming at the top of her lungs, announcing to the whole equestrian center she had arrived. It got worse when Scarlett saw the horses. She turned into Cujo, baring her teeth and straining with every muscle to pull away from me. God only knows what she would have done if she had gotten loose. Probably nothing. The safety of the leash made her brave.

Luckily, the horses were not being shown at the moment of her arrival or we would have been thrown out. They were, however, standing in line, awaiting the next presentation. They all witnessed Scarlett's behavior and showed signs of agitation, neighing and kicking up their hind legs as their riders tried to calm them. *It's too late to turn back*, I thought. *Just keep heading toward the adoption area.* I assumed that once we got there, she would settle down. Oh boy, was I wrong!

Usually I put up signs around the arena saying dogs were up for adoption near the food vendor. Then I would set up a chair in the shady area and spread a blanket for the dogs with their water bowl on top. But today was different. I obviously couldn't walk around putting up signs or do anything else with my hands, other than holding onto her and Andy. I was very upset, and I was starting to get really mad as well. My arm was shaking from trying to restrain the lunatic Terrier, and my hand was throbbing. I had also broken into an extreme sweat—the kind I had not experienced since living in Florida during the torrid summer months. I sat on her leash to give my hand a few moments break, but I didn't have much control, so I held on again and watched as the leash cut into my hand, making it throb even more and turn red. It was one of the worst twenty minutes I have ever experienced. I was so upset I wanted to cry.

Normally, people who wanted to see the dogs up for adoption surrounded me, and by the end of the day, I usually had a great prospective home for at least one dog. But today, no one came near or offered to help, as Scarlett nearly pulled my arm off, wailing and lurching at any animal that walked by. And there were a lot of them. Dogs and horses everywhere!

I'm 5'2", and at that time, I was 100-pounds. I simply did not have the strength to hold onto this insane energy much longer. My dilemma was immediate: how would I get her out safely without ruining the horse show, which by now had started? It seemed like Scarlett would kill any dog that came near her, except for the Hound named Andy who she tried to get to join in with her, but he was too mellow and smart for that kind of behavior. He only looked at me with terror in his eyes as if to say, "Can you believe this?" I was grateful he was a calm and mature dog. She, however, was in the truest sense *a nightmare on a leash*!

I had brought a blanket in a bag along with my purse. The bag was still on my shoulder on Andy's side. I wrapped his leash around my arm and slowly and awkwardly reached up and pulled the blanket from the bag. Scarlett seemed slightly tired from all her antics and was panting heavily, though it didn't stop her from searching for another victim. Her eyes, full of fear and anxiety, darted back and forth. I geared myself up for what I was about to do, praying it would work. I took a few deep breaths, threw the blanket over Scarlett's head, and grabbed hold of it under her chin so that it covered her eyes. Then I ran! I dragged those two dogs as fast as I could back the way we came, past the people, and the dogs, and horses, with Scarlett doing everything she could to get her head out, but she didn't make a sound.

I don't remember taking notice of how anyone responded to this sight. I just ran straight ahead, back to the car. I opened the door as fast as I could, and I pushed Scarlett into the backseat. Andy jumped in behind her, and I tied them to the door handle and slammed the car door. I always tie dogs' leashes inside the car. That way, when I open the door they can't bolt. This is always a good idea, but in Scarlett's case it was vital.

I thought my arm was going to fall off! I was in so much pain, as stressed out as I had ever been, and on the verge of tears. Not only because of how hard it had been dealing with her, but also how hard it was going to be to find her a home. "I don't know who is going to want her!" I announced to the employees, when we got back to the store. "You were right. She's a nightmare on a leash!"

A few weeks later, Scarlett was still at Pet Mania. Andy had gotten a home with the man and his wife who had come in that first day, so there was no need for me to have brought him to the equestrian center. If I had only known that home was going to work out, I would have had two hands to handle the wild Terrier that day.

As time went on, there had been tons of interest in Scarlett. But once people walked the leash-aggressive canine they changed their minds. I remember sitting in front of her pen wondering how I could help her. I had heard about a trainer who took dogs into his facility and worked with them. His fee was $1,000 and he supposedly was very good. I had been working steadily on TV at that point and had money saved. *Why don't I do what that woman in New York did? Why don't I pay to help this dog?*

Two days later, with my check in hand, I drove Scarlett to the trainer's facility in East Los Angeles, where she would be staying for three weeks. I felt good that I had the money to help her. *But this better help*, I thought, as I handed my $1,000 check over to the nice looking trainer.

"You can come by and see how well she's doing," he said to me a week later. "She's come a long way."

The next day I drove there to see what I had hoped would be a miraculous change. As I pulled into the parking lot, I could see Scarlett through the fence. She was tied to a pole, while the other dogs were behind another fence. She sat very still and calm watching them. That all changed when I came toward her. Scarlett acted like I was her long lost mama who she hadn't seen for ten years. It warmed my heart to know that the Terrier knew I was helping her.

I would love to say that the $1,000 and the three weeks changed Scarlett's leash aggression, but that's not exactly what happened. Yes, she could sit and watch the dogs inside the compound, and she was a *bit* better on leash in the world. But she was still Scarlett.

Pet Mania did not want her back, so I was going to have to board her. Thankfully, I got a call a few days before she was to be released from the trainer. The call came from an ad I had placed on Petfinder.com, a website for animals that need homes.

"Hi, my name is Suzanne, and I'm calling about Scarlett," a sweet voice said on my machine. I remember I was sitting at home on the first landing of my green-carpeted stairs looking out of the sliding glass door when I called her back. This was Sammy and Mazie's usual spot to lie on. That part of the stairway felt like a cocoon, and I needed to feel secure in the hope that this call might bring forth a miracle. I didn't think this innocent-sounding woman could handle Scarlett, but it was worth a try. I sat on that step, prayed, and dialed: "Yes, she's still available, and yes, she is the cutest thing in the world."

"She's nothing like my last dog, but there was something about her that called to me," Suzanne swooned.

I told her everything. I divulged all of Scarlett's sweetness and her nightmarish behavior.

"I think I still want to meet her, and I think I could handle that."

"She actually loves dogs, just not on a leash," I told her.

"So I could take her to the dog park, without a problem?"

"Absolutely."

"Then I would definitely like to meet her."

Wow, I thought as I hung up the phone, but I was afraid to get too excited. That weekend Scarlett and I drove to Suzanne's house for the meeting and home check. I had never heard of Sun Valley before and wondered what it would be like. As I pulled up to Suzanne's town house gate, I did not notice a lot of dogs walking in the neighborhood. *That's a good sign*, I thought as I breathed a sigh of relief. I parked the car and got Scarlett out of the backseat. "Be on your best behavior, little miss. This could be your only chance for a home."

We got out of the car; Scarlett glanced at me quickly and led the way to Suzanne, who was waiting outside her front door.

"Hi, Scarlett." She smiled and reached out to pet her possible new companion. "And hi, Sylva. Thanks for bringing her."

Scarlett pushed herself into Suzanne's town house without waiting to be invited. She then sniffed her way around inside before going out to the patio and fixating on the birds and squirrels in the trees behind the complex.

"There's a doggy door, so she can go in and out when I'm at work and can keep herself busy watching all the wildlife out there."

I measured the gap in the fence to make sure it was not big enough for Scarlett to squeeze out. Luckily, it wasn't. I spent the next hour with the two of them worrying that, once Suzanne got a load of Scarlett in wild action, she would not want to keep her.

"Do you want to go for a walk to see what she's like before I leave?" I asked Suzanne.

"No, why don't we just let her settle in tonight, and I'll take her out tomorrow and let you know."

Before I left, I showed Suzanne how to walk the leash-aggressive dog with the soft choke chain, prong collar, and two leashes. I didn't sleep very much that night. The thought of putting Scarlett into boarding the next day when she was returned was not something I was looking forward to.

In the morning the phone rang, and I held my breath as I answered it. "Well, you weren't kidding. She's a nightmare on a leash," Suzanne said.

My heart sank. "I know. Sorry, I'll be there . . ."

"But if I put a halter on as well I think I can handle her. I think it will work."

I couldn't believe it! A miracle had happened! I wanted to reach through the phone and hug her! "Great! Are you sure?"

A year later I went to visit. Scarlett almost knocked me down when I entered the house, as she smothered me with kisses. "She doesn't act like that with anyone, not even me," Suzanne said.

"She's thanking me for giving her the life she has with you," I explained. I had seen this happen a few times by then. Owners always thought the dogs loved me more, but that wasn't the case. It was that they knew I had saved them, one way or another, and put them in their loving homes, and that is why they were so happy to see me.

Years later, Scarlett had to have an eye removed because of a disease. Then, a few years after that, she got very sick and had to be put down. Suzanne was devastated. The Terrier was her life and her love.

CHAPTER EIGHT

So Now You're a Dog Rescuer?

I was with my dear friend, Adel, at the Sand Bar on Anna Maria Island—a cozy restaurant on the Gulf of Mexico, a few blocks from the rock house I had lived in as a young girl, and on the same strip of beach where I had learned to swim. My mother had moved us there when I was six, the year she left my father and drove my twin sister, and brother, and me from New York to the island in Florida she remembered as a child.

Adel and I had met in Los Angeles when I lived there the first time. Coincidentally, she ended up moving to Florida, a few miles away from the island where I had spent the best three years of my childhood and where I return every summer.

"Are you just going to give up your career?" Adel asked. "You're the one we all thought would make it to the top. And that's what you always wanted. Why are you rescuing dogs?"

I laughed at what I knew most of my friends were thinking. "First of all, I'm not giving up my career. I'm still a working actress, and as long as I'm in the game, anything can happen."

My free-spirited friend looked at me with her piercing blue eyes and smiled. "Well, I just hope you're happy."

I gazed out at the water and envisioned my six-year-old self in her red-and-white, one-piece bathing suit, learning to swim. The white sand sparkled in the sunlight, while the blue-green waves lapped at the shore. The island was home to me. A feeling I treasured. A feeling I thought everyone deserved to have, including dogs—a safe, loving, wonderful, forever home. "I'm an actress and it's what I love," I said to Adel. "But I need to serve another purpose here as well, and I think rescuing is it."

I had come to believe that we should all have a purpose for being here, but that some of us were meant to do more than one thing. So back in LA I tried daily to manage what was thrown at me, and for a while there, it was dog after dog. Every time I left the house for an audition or a job, I would pray I didn't see a dog in need on the street. At that point, I was finding them constantly. Some had gotten out of their yards, while others were discarded strays. People would say to me, "Where do you see these dogs? I never see any dogs on the street." I saw them all the time and would stop to get them.

Sometimes it was quick and easy. Other times, if they were afraid, I would spend hours or days trying to loop a leash around their necks and get them into my car. Then I would return them to their owners if the dogs came from a good home, or I would find them a new one. In hindsight, I realize I was so focused on helping dogs that the universe kept putting them in front of me, and not only on the streets. I would get calls from people who had heard I was rescuing and needed help finding a new home for their own dog for one reason or another—usually for reasons that I didn't feel were good enough, like having a baby and not wanting their four-legged child anymore.

I had turned into the very woman who years before had intrigued me—the woman in New York who spent her money helping dogs.

Because the legal limit for owning animals is three in Los Angeles and Burbank, I very rarely brought my rescues home. Occasionally, I kept one overnight, but most of the time I put them in boarding, which was expensive, or found a foster, which was never easy.

The majority of the dogs I rescued were not spayed, neutered or microchipped, so I had to pay for that as well as shots. And some of them were sick and needed medical care, so I was spending thousands, and thousands, and thousands of dollars a year rescuing animals. The adoption fees I charged covered only a small percentage of the cost, but the highest stress came not from the money or the dogs, but from dealing with the people.

I would get calls like this one: "Hi, Sylva. Well, I don't think we are going to be able to keep Harry. He doesn't seem to like our dog."

"Well, it's only been two days. You have to give it time."

"I know. I'm just worried we made the wrong decision. Maybe we should not have gotten a second dog."

"You didn't make the wrong decision. Give it time. They will become best friends. I've seen it happen over and over."

"I'm just worried . . ."

"Don't worry! Give it time. How would you feel if you moved to a new home with new people? You would have to adjust as well. It's the same thing. Give it time."

Most people would heed my advice, but the energy I had to spend to get them to "give it time," no matter what the problem, was exhausting.

The day after I left any dog at their new home, I would call to check in, holding my breath as I asked, "So how's it going?" Usually, after the first two weeks with no problems, I could assume the adoption was final. But that wasn't always the case.

As an actress, I had been studying people for years. I knew human behavior very well, or at least I *thought* I did, until I started rescuing.

You can tell a lot about a person by the way they care for their animals. Such was the extreme case of a wonderful couple who adopted a Shepherd, only to find out a week later that the dog needed $5,000 worth of surgery because of a twisted intestine. "We can take a loan out," I remember them saying. "She's our dog now, so she's our responsibility. We wouldn't think of sending her back or asking you to help us. You do enough."

And then there was the lovely woman who said, "I'd like to adopt another dog because mine is lonely while I'm at work."

There are also other kinds of people, like the lady who dumped her adorable little Yorkie on Hollywood Boulevard because he chewed up one of her shoes, and the man who took his two-year-old Jack Russell in to the vet to have him euthanized because he destroyed his cordless phone. And then there was the guy who called me about adopting a Pitbull I rescued—for his girlfriend.

"Does she have any other dogs?" I asked.

"No. She had three, but two of them ran away. The other one was hit by a car and died."

There was silence. Then I laughed aloud. "Are you serious?"

"Yes."

"And you think I'm going to adopt to *her*?"

A Pitbull that was rescued by a friend of mine was on the news because the dog was hurt terribly and then dumped out of a car. People came out of the woodwork to donate money toward the dog's recovery, hoping to adopt if he pulled through. A few celebrities got involved to raise money as well, which was great. But I was reminded of the time that I stood in the Louvre Museum in Paris and watched while a crowd of people gathered in front of the Mona Lisa. The celebrated work of art is surrounded by walls of truly beautiful Renaissance paintings which no one paid any attention to. They only wanted to see the famous lady.

So if it takes getting a dog on TV or the Internet to raise awareness about the world of rescue, my hope is that *every* day an animal in need is brought to the public's attention.

There is a huge underground movement. Every day, hundreds of e-mails circulate around the Internet pleading with people to rescue dogs and cats about to be put to sleep. I have rescued or re-homed about twenty cats myself, as well as a horse or two.

Like a good matchmaker, a rescuer should get to know each animal to make sure they are placed with the right person or people. For instance: a household with physically active owners if the dog is a high-energy breed; or proper fences if the animal is a jumper or darter. And the adopter must be savvy and in control if the dog has a tendency to be alpha with another canine in the new environment, or vice versa. And, of course—first and foremost—all the animals should be placed in a loving home where they will live inside and their needs, such as exercise and a warm bed, will be met.

A good rescuer also will have the adopter sign a contract that stipulates the animal must be returned to the rescuer at any time, if the adopter can no longer keep the dog or cat. Each animal's microchip should stay in the rescuer's name, with the adopter listed as the secondary contact. That way, if the adopter decides to drop the dog or cat off at a shelter, violating the agreement to give the animal back, the rescuer will be notified.

I have a contract and I have always taken animals back. Except Samantha.

Samantha was a four-year-old Rottweiler/Beagle that I rescued on her last day at the North Central Los Angeles Animal Shelter. She was a backyard dog that had been turned in by her owner. Her beautiful brown eyes stared back at me from the picture in the email. I had rescued numerous dogs from death row by then and was usually drawn to the Shepherd and Rottweiler mixes, the bigger dogs that had less of a chance of being saved.

The email claimed Samantha was dog-friendly. But, when I read it, I got a weird feeling that she really was not dog-friendly. I had no reason to think this; it was just an intuition. As it turned out, I was right.

This sweet, 50-pound, Rottweiler/Beagle mix turned into a mean girl the second she spotted another dog. At first, I thought it was just a leash thing as with Scarlett, but once I got Samantha into the foster home, I was actually afraid to let her off leash. She started baring her teeth, as though she was getting ready for the fight of her life. Needless to say, I did not leave her there. I placed her in a boarding facility where, after her first night, the management informed me that, not only was Samantha *not* dog friendly, but she could also jump a six-foot fence in an instant. Thankfully there had been no canines on the other side of the wall when she scaled it, as there would have been a fight.

I ultimately ended up paying for a year of boarding and training at another facility for her. Every weekend, I would drive an hour to pick her up and another hour to get her to adoptions, all the while actively looking for a home for her during the week. Many people wanted Samantha, because she was beautiful and so well behaved, but they either had other dogs or six-foot fences.

A year later, my friend Simon, who lived in an apartment, offered to foster her, but he couldn't keep her because he would be leaving the country.

A few months after Samantha went to live with Simon, I had a vision of who would adopt her. That sometimes happened with me and the dogs. Before I placed them, I would allow myself to imagine who the owner would be—not only to imagine what kind of home the dog should go to, but the type of person as well. When I tried this with Samantha, for some reason I saw her with a gay man or a gay couple. So I set about trying to make that happen.

I asked one of my friends for the names of gay magazines in which I could place an advertisement. He suggested I go to the Silver Spoon restaurant on Santa Monica Boulevard (which no longer exists) to check the magazine racks that lined the street. I did, and when I found a magazine that felt right, I placed an ad for Samantha in it. I got one call.

"Hi, I'm calling about Samantha."

"Yes!"

"Did she find a home yet?"

"No!"

"My dog died recently. Samantha looks a lot like her."

"Do you have any other animals right now?"

"No. I wasn't really thinking of getting another dog so soon, but I saw her picture—"

"Where do you live?"

"Las Vegas."

VEGAS! SHIT! "Vegas . . . Okay, that's not that far. Do you have a house or—?"

"I own a town house."

"Is there a yard?"

"Unfortunately, no, but—"

"No, that's great! No yard is good." *No yard. No fence to jump.* "What do you do in Vegas?" He sounded like a nice, responsible guy.

"I do a show there that I've been in for years, so I'm around during the day and she wouldn't be alone a lot."

It was too good to be true. "You know she's not good with other animals. I put that in the ad."

"Yeah, that's fine. I'm not around other animals so it wouldn't be a problem."

The next day I called a woman who lived in Las Vegas and Big Bear, California, and had adopted a Pitbull from a rescue friend of mine. Ironically, she had called about Samantha from a flyer I had put up in Big Bear a few months before, while I was doing a home check there for another dog. The woman already had a dog, but wanted a friend for him. Since Samantha could not be with other dogs, I suggested the Pitbull, Nundi, who loved other dogs. She agreed to meet him and ultimately adopted him. I knew she would do the home check for me, and I trusted her completely. She and her husband were huge animal lovers. After the home check was completed, I got the call: "He's great. A super nice guy with a beautiful, safe town house."

The next weekend, Jude, Samantha, and I were on our way to Sin City. After meeting her new daddy and seeing his place, we felt assured that Samantha had her forever, safe, loving home.

Months later, I got a call from the guy saying that his friend had fallen in love with Samantha and wanted her. The guy had decided to move and she had been staying at his friend's house for the last month. Now the friend did not want to give her up. The guy felt it was meant to be and wanted to know if that would be okay. His friend had a house with nine-foot fences, ran with her every day, and allowed Samantha to sleep in his bed. After talking to the friend, I gave my okay and sent him an adoption contract to sign. Since Samantha had already been with him for a month, I knew the home was safe.

Four years later, I got a call.

"Hi, Sylva, I have some bad news. Samantha attacked my friend's dog. I can't keep her anymore."

"What do you mean she attacked a dog? How did you allow her to get close to another dog?"

There was a long pause.

"My friend came to live with me. He has two dogs and Samantha had been fine with them for the last few months, but yesterday she turned on one of them."

I was stunned, heartbroken, and pissed as hell. "Why did you bring other dogs into your house when you knew she was dog aggressive?"

"Well, she *was* okay with them—"

"She's *not* good with other dogs! That's why it took me a stressful year and thousands of dollars to find her what I thought was the right home."

"Well, if you don't take her back I'm going to put her to sleep."

He expected me to jump in my car after four years and drive to Vegas all because he had set Samantha up to fail. I was furious and so sad for that dear, dear dog.

I decided to call his bluff, as I thought he loved Samantha and would not go through with his threat. "I *can't* take her back," I said. "I can't afford to board her because I'm paying for three other dogs' boarding costs right now. Besides, the worst thing for her would be to go back to living in a kennel (which was true). If you really don't want her you'd better go ahead and put her to sleep. But whatever you do, don't just dump her at a shelter, because they're strangers and will put her down anyway. If she's going to be put down, someone she knows and trusts ought to be the one to do it." When he didn't reply, I softened a bit. "Look. Let me make some calls and see if there's anyone I know who can take her, someone who has an apartment and no other dogs."

I was terribly upset when I hung up. I had spent so much time, energy, and money on that dog to make sure she was going to her forever, loving home and now this!

I reached out to his friend, the original guy in Vegas who I had adopted her to, but for some unknown reason he couldn't take her. I could not find anyone else either. The last time I spoke to Samantha's owner, he told me he was going to keep her separate from the other dogs. I have now since been told that he gave her to a coworker, who had no other dogs. Who knows if that's true because, when I asked to call the person, no number was given to me. After that, he would not respond to my calls or emails.

To this day, I am torn about Samantha. I feel I let her down. Though I felt responsible for her, the person who had her for four years needed to feel responsible, needed to do the right thing, which he did not. He set her up to fail. My only consolation was knowing that she had four great years of love, kindness, exercise, and a warm bed. All the things she had not known before I rescued her, as she had been a backyard dog.

Samantha is just one story, one journey of a dog that was not wanted and then thought she had found her forever home. In the shelter system, where between five and six million animals are killed a year, there are millions like her and millions more that never even get a chance to know what a safe, loving home feels like.

CHAPTER NINE

"Spycial" Charlie—Part II

Sometimes the universe aligns to save a dog. Not all of the time, but sometimes. I had been home for two days from filming a movie of the week and was heading back out of town that weekend to finish shooting. The sun was shining into my second floor home office, bouncing off the yellow paint, filling the room with rays of golden light. I glanced out the window to see a line of horses going by below, with riders on their backs. These daily occurrences on the path gave me great joy. It was the reason I had chosen to live in the equestrian area.

Sammy, Mazie, and Beau Bo were spread out around the floor on their beds, peacefully sleeping after our morning playtime in the field behind our house. I looked at them one by one, smiling at the good fortune they all had to be our dogs and to live such a great life. I did that every day as I counted my own blessings.

Suddenly, I was startled by the phone ringing. I turned to look at the caller ID. It was my husband Jude. "Hi, honey," I said.

"My Princess, listen. My brother just called to tell me that Charlie is at that horrible, high-kill shelter in New York."

"What? The CACC?" The same shelter I had read about in *New York* magazine so many years before.

"He bit the kid at the home you put him in. Evidently, the kid has been tormenting him all these years. He finally snapped, bit him, and the parents didn't know what else to do because they thought the kid would kill him. They're devastated."

"What?" I repeated.

"My brother just happened to be in the city today, called his friend, who told him what happened."

"Oh my god!" My peaceful beautiful morning was destroyed. "What exactly happened?"

"Evidently, this kid is a bit off," Jude informed me.

"He's not even a kid. He was seventeen when I put Charlie there, so he must be twenty-one by now!"

"Well, he has been annoying Charlie for years, though I'm not sure exactly what he did, but the dog snapped and now he's going to be put to sleep."

Jude gave me the number to the family. I calmed down and called them.

"Hi, it's Sylva. I heard what happened. Can you tell me Charlie's impound number at the shelter? I'm going to get him out," I told her.

"I don't know if they'll release him," the distraught mother gasped. "They said that—"

"Please, just give me the number, and I'll take care of it. Don't worry. I'll let you know."

I immediately called Marilyn in New York, the rescuer I got Sammy from. She gave me the phone number of a woman she knew who worked at the shelter. That lady told me that Charlie was there, that she had tested him, that he seemed like a great dog, and she couldn't believe that he had bitten someone. However, because he had, they couldn't put him up for adoption, which meant he would be euthanized. "Why don't you call the head of the shelter to see if he can help," the woman suggested.

"Hi, my name is Sylva Kelegian," I said to his secretary. "I need to talk to your boss about a dog in your possession. It's a very important matter."

I guess I sounded extremely serious because the shelter head was on the phone within a minute. "How can I help you?" he said.

"Hi. I'm calling about a dog that you have named Charlie." I then gave him the impound number. "I rescued this dog four years ago and placed him with what I thought was a wonderful family. The kid in the home was seventeen at the time of placement and now I have found out he has been tormenting the dog for the last four years. I guess Charlie finally snapped and bit him. The parents love the dog but were afraid the kid would kill him so they brought him to you. Now they regret it. We want to get him out. My husband and I are willing to fly Charlie to Los Angeles so you won't have any further responsibility, if you could release him."

There was a long pause. Finally, the man replied. "I'm in charge here, and I say what happens to the dogs, not you."

Did I really just hear that? "I know you're in charge, so I'm asking you to release him and we will fly him to Los Angeles so you don't have any—"

"Please don't tell me how to do my job, Ma'am. Have a good day." And then he hung up. I sat at my desk stunned, shaking from anger, and absolutely shocked! *Who did this man think he was—God?* I called the woman at the shelter back who had met Charlie. "He hung up on me. He fucking hung up on me!"

"Yeah, I'm not surprised. He likes the power he has here."

"What can I do?" I wailed.

She thought for a minute. "Let me give you his email and try emailing him. Marilyn says you're an actress and a rescuer. Maybe that will make him change his mind, if you know what I mean."

I did. I knew exactly what she meant.

My email went something like this: "Hi. We spoke today about Charlie, until you hung up the phone on me. I'm writing to ask you to please release him tomorrow. I will have someone pick him up and put him on a plane to Los Angeles so that you have no legal repercussions if he were to bite again. I am an actress in Los Angeles and very involved in the rescue community out here. I would hate to have to go to the press with this story. Knowing how many animals the CACC puts down, I'm sure you don't need bad publicity. Please respond to my request ASAP so that I can make the arrangements for getting Charlie on a plane to LA. Thank you very much. Sylva Kelegian."

I got a call within the hour from his secretary. "You can have someone pick up the animal by five p.m. today," she said.

Charlie's owners got him out of the shelter and brought him to their friend's apartment, where the mother slept on the floor with the scared dog that night. She loved him very much and was devastated. The next day, they brought him to the airport.

It felt like *déjà vu*, waiting for Charlie to be unloaded at the pickup area. After all, it was just three years before that we had done the same thing, holding our breath, waiting for our princess. And then, there he was! His beautiful, black face staring out from the huge crate we had paid for to ship him in. He was terrified. I could see it in his wide eyes. "Spycial Charlie," I called out to him. "Hi, big guy."

"Hey, Charlie," Jude said in a soothing voice. "How are you?"

I got my nylon choke and leash ready as I cracked open the door of the crate and quickly slipped the collar over his head. He had to pee badly so I ran him over to the grass, where he relieved himself for what seemed like minutes. As he did, I put a regular collar and tag on him that I had prepared before he arrived. He looked at me and I smiled. But I was heartbroken. He was not the same dog I had left with the family that day. The light had gone out of his eyes.

When he was done peeing, he nuzzled his head between my legs and stood there. I reached down to pet his gorgeous, thick, black fur. "It's going to be okay now, Spycial Charlie," I said. "I'll never let anyone hurt you again."

If my brother-in-law had not been in New York to call his friend that day, if I had not been at home or unable to reach out to the shelter, Charlie would have been killed. We could never get a straight answer about what the boy had done to him. "Oh, you know, you should just let sleeping dogs lie," was all the father would say. My brother-in-law told me that they were embarrassed and truly sorry about what had happened. But whatever their son did, they were not telling me.

Because I was leaving town to finish shooting the TV show, we put Charlie in a boarding facility until I got back. Jude was not up for handling four dogs in the town house on his own, and I had to make sure Charlie was going to be okay with our three.

"He's really sad and confused. He doesn't know where he is or why. I feel terrible for him," my husband said the first day I called from the set. Jude went every day to walk him, so he wouldn't have to be in a kennel all day.

"I know it is not ideal now, but once I get back he can stay with us until we find him the right home," I assured him.

Our plan was not to keep Charlie, because we had three dogs already, and he was a highly placeable animal. Beautiful and sweet, good with other dogs, and in the right hands, he would have a great life.

My first night back, I incorporated Charlie into our household and he did well. But when I asked him to come upstairs to go to bed, he wouldn't. I reached out for his collar and he growled at me. "No! That is not okay! No!" I firmly told him. I sounded very angry and in control, but actually I was scared. I had never had a dog growl at me before, except Sammy over food when she was a puppy. I left him alone to sleep downstairs that night, but I was beginning to see the damage that had been done. He was tired of being pushed and pulled and told what to do. I decided to give him his space, but he could never growl at me again.

Charlie got along with all of our dogs, but because he had lived with a deaf Boxer who could not hear his warning growls when he was agitated, he would strike out and bite—not hard, just a warning bite, but hard enough to give Mazie and Beau Bo little puncture wounds.

After a few weeks of letting him settle down, I decided to take him to adoptions. He got tons of attention, but I had to be careful who I placed him with—a home with no kids and only responsible adults who knew his background.

I called Charlie's previous family to get a little more information and spoke to the father. "You know how boys can be? Our son never left him alone and always bothered him when he was sleeping or wanted some space," he said.

"Yes, but what did he actually do to him?"

"I don't really know. I was never there," he admitted.

When I realized Charlie's issues were being nudged and pushed and God only knows what else, I hired a trainer. She suggested I get him a basket muzzle so I could feed him a treat through the wire bars every time I pushed or pulled him a little. We were trying to desensitize him to turn it into a positive experience, which worked.

By then Jude and I had decided to keep him. Beau Bo was old and not going to be around much longer, and we realized we couldn't put Charlie in a situation where someone could press his buttons and he might bite again. It would not be fair to anyone.

One day, Meredith, a rescue friend of mine, cut Charlie's nails, and he bit her arm badly. We all had our doubts. Could we trust this dog? The answer was, yes. It was our fault that we had not muzzled him before cutting his nails. I'd never had any of the dogs' nails trimmed at home before, but Meredith seemed to know what she was doing so I had let her. We both learned a big lesson that day—to always muzzle a dog when you cut their nails, unless you're positive they are okay with it. Charlie ran out to the patio when I screamed at the top of my lungs, but the damage had been done. Meredith's arm was terribly punctured, and I had to rush her to the hospital. Charlie knew he had done wrong. Our troubled canine cried and pawed at the glass door when I closed it on him. He seemed to be saying, "I thought she was hurting me, and I had to stop her. I'm sorry. I didn't mean it."

"Where did you get that bite?" the doctor asked when he came into the room. "Looks like a bad one."

"We were trying to get a dog on the street and it bit me and ran away," Meredith said. Luckily she was a rescuer and knew that dog bites, legally, had to be reported by doctors to animal control, so that the canine could be quarantined for ten days.

The doctor looked at the two of us, a little smirk forming at the side of his mouth. "Well . . . just make sure you don't try to catch him again."

The first five years of Charlie's life had not been good but, with us, he was happy, loved, and safe. He adored his family, and every day I could see the gratitude in his eyes. I had saved him twice and he knew it. I still felt bad that, because of me, he'd been in that second home, which hadn't turned out as I had hoped. Still, he seemed to know what we had done for him, and he was very grateful and loyal. Our dear Shepherd/Akita enjoyed his long walks with Jude every day, and when I took him on hikes, he would not stray far. I could always count on Charlie coming back to check on me, rubbing up against my leg, and making eye contact before he took off again. At night, our big black boy would stay up late with my husband and lie at the front door, protecting us from the outside world. When Jude came to bed, he would follow.

A year later we decided to buy a house. Walking our dogs four times a day was wearing us both out. It was the height of the real estate market, so we sold our town house and were able to get double the price we had paid for it. We then purchased a three-bedroom home with a big backyard, and I began the process of remodeling the house inside and out.

Super Pooh or Pooh Bear, as Charlie was now nicknamed, could not stand loud noises. They scared the hell out of him. So when, a few years later, we decided to enclose the patio, he would hide in my husband's office and shake. Jude's brother, Tom, had recently moved to Los Angeles and was living down the street. To relieve Charlie's stress, I would drop him off at my brother-in-law's apartment in the morning, with Mazie for company. My husband then took them out to relieve themselves in the afternoon. Then they would come home at night after the workers left. This went on for a few weeks, but Charlie seemed to be weak and terrified when he came back to our house. On his walks, he was not his peppy self.

Jude took him to our veterinarian who prescribed him Valium. "He's just stressed. He'll be okay," the vet said.

But our dog was not okay. A few days later, he couldn't get up off the floor. I had to stay home because the construction guys were working, so my husband carried Pooh to the car and took him back to the vet. After some X-rays were done, we found out his spleen had burst. Evidently, Charlie had been sick, and the stress from the re-modeling exacerbated it. We had two options: put him through a $4,000 surgery, which did not guarantee anything and most likely would not save his life because he was too far gone, or put him to sleep. If our Charles did survive the surgery, he would have a long, unpleasant recovery.

We decided to bring Charlie home and hire a vet to come to our house and put him to sleep that evening. Having our boy (who had been through so much) experience any more distress in his life was not an option. We were given painkillers so that he would rest easily until then. But as the hour came upon us, I called and cancelled. Never having put a dog to sleep before, I could not do it to our beloved Pooh. "Maybe he'll be okay by the morning? If he's not, then we'll bring him in? All right?" I said to Jude. I was in total denial that the first dog I had ever rescued was dying.

"I don't think he's going to be okay, but we'll see," my husband sighed.

I slept with Charlie on the floor of our bedroom and held him tight. In the middle of the night, I awoke and thought he was trying to get up, but it was just his reflexes. At six a.m., I woke up again to a gurgling sound. It was as if he was drowning, which he was—in his own blood. "Jude, wake up. He's going. Our Charles is going!"

We surrounded him: Jude, Sammy, Mazie, Beau Bo, and I, holding him close as he took his last breath. It was awful, the worst thing I had ever experienced. To witness our beloved dog choking to death on his own blood—after all the hardship in his life—was heartbreaking. I felt it was unfair, that it was my fault. I should have put him to sleep hours before, but we hadn't known he could choke to death.

Jude and I wrapped Charlie in a blanket for the drive to the crematory, where we picked out a beautiful urn. My husband sobbed for three days straight. Our other dogs were confused and sad. I was a wreck and felt terribly guilty. Though I had saved Spycial Charlie from a bad situation, I had also put him into another one, only to make his last day on earth hell.

I would never let another dog suffer again.

CHAPTER TEN

South Central

The month before South Central, I had completed a Stephen King movie of the week called *Desperation*, for which I had been paid very well. I hate to travel for work because I have no choice where I'm going, and the odds are high I will encounter an animal in need on location. This time I was in Bisbee, Arizona, a small mining town.

My second day there, as I was walking around the hilly streets, I saw a Pitbull running in a junkyard with some puppies. The mother of the puppies, I was soon to find out, was an adorable little Shepherd mix who was living on the attached property with a guy and his black female Corgi mix. After a few days of passing the property and realizing that none of the dogs were fixed, I started talking to the owner, who was well meaning but not aware that he needed to spay and neuter his dogs. "They're not all mine," he said to me that first day. "My friend is in jail and the Pit and the Shepherd are his. She just gave birth on my property."

"Would you mind if I got her spayed and the Pit neutered? I'm going to be here for ten days. That way you don't have to worry about having more unwanted puppies."

He seemed to mull this suggestion over very seriously. "Well, I don't know what my friend would say about that. But he's going to be in jail for a while, so maybe I just won't tell him."

"Good idea," I assured him. "And can I come by to walk the two girl dogs in the afternoon? I take a long walk every day that I'm sure they would love and I could use the company." The girls were kept in a filthy, dirty, cramped area near a trailer, while the Pit daddy and puppies had a huge area to roam on the upper property.

He mulled this suggestion even longer than my first one, but eventually he agreed. We were shooting in Bisbee because of the mines. My scenes were shot at night and mostly outside. I played the mother of the lead boy, and in the middle of the show, I get taken over by the evil force and I turn into the scary monster.

Every afternoon after I woke up, I would take the Shepherd mix and the Corgi mix on a long hike, which they looked forward to after the first day. They acted like prisoners being released from jail, jumping on me and howling when I came through the gate in anticipation of being let out of their cell.

That week, I got the mama and the daddy fixed. Though I offered to take them all back to LA with me to find them great homes when I left, the man allowed me to take only the Pit daddy and the puppies. I had to leave the girls behind, and that was hard for them and me. I opted to drive back to LA instead of flying first class, which the production company pays for, so I could take the dogs with me. I had set up a foster home for the Pit and had reached out to another rescuer who was waiting for the puppies on arrival. They were put into a great home together the next week, and the foster for the Pit daddy ended up adopting him.

A few weeks after I was back, I went to the dentist. The very efficient and warm dental assistant smiled as she came into the room. With her beautiful pearly whites sparkling, she said, "Sylva, I know you're an actress, but I heard you tell the doc last time you were here that you rescue dogs. Is that true?"

My gut tightened. I knew where this was going. I had just placed the Bisbee animals and was rescue-dog-free. I now wanted to focus a bit on myself and spend some of my time and money on *me*. "Yes?" I cautiously said.

"Well, I live in South Central. Where I live, they're a lot of dogs on the streets. But there is one dog in particular that I'm concerned about, a Chow mix who has been sitting on the corner next to her dead puppy who was hit by a car. It's really sad, and I don't know what to do. She also has two more puppies who live behind a house across the street from me."

Not just one, but three!

The next day, I drove to South Central to see the dogs. I had not been to South Central since the Rodney King riots years before when I had gone to help serve food. The stores and restaurants were not open at that time because of the riots, so people were hungry. Back then, it was a dirty, treeless, depressed area.

This South Central was very different from the one I remembered. I was struck at how nicely the homes were kept, including beautifully manicured lawns. However, it seemed odd because all of the houses had bars on the windows, as if people lived in their own secure prisons.

The mama dog was nowhere to be found, and a woman who lived on the block told me that animal control had picked up the dead puppy, but could not get the mother. "There are two more who live in the back of that empty house," she said, pointing to the home next door.

"Are they friendly? Will they come up to you?"

"No. They're wild dogs."

Great, just what I need, two feral puppies to deal with, I thought. A feral animal is unsocialized and will not come near people, which makes them very difficult to catch.

I walked around the house and into the backyard. The front gate had been torn down, which made it easy to access. There was junk everywhere: old cars, lawnmowers, pipes, windows, and pieces of wood.

Suddenly I froze. The cutest puppy I had ever seen in my life stared at me from across the yard, then bolted under an old car. He was red, like a little red, short-coated bear, with black eyes. I looked under the car from across the yard and saw him huddled up next to a small Shepherd mix puppy. They stared back at me with terrified looks in their eyes. Unfortunately, this was before I knew about and owned a dog trap, which would have been the fastest way to catch the dogs.

How the hell am I going to get these dogs? I wondered. All three sides of the fence had holes everywhere, which made it easy for the puppies to escape. Plus, the driveway had no gate to block that exit.

I walked back to my car, got a bag of dog food, and left it in the front yard near the scraps the neighbors had been feeding them. They had also put out a bowl of water, which I refreshed from a hose across the street.

"Did you see them?" the woman next door asked me as I was contemplating my next move.

"Yes, they're adorable, but very scared," I said. "I'm going to have to come back tomorrow and board everything up to trap them. Here's my number. If you see the mother dog, please call me right away."

I assumed the mother was probably *not* feral, but dumped or escaped from a backyard. It would be easier to capture her, making it more likely for me to attract her puppies.

"I'll call you if I see her," the woman said. "I'll be around tomorrow if you need me."

"Thank you." I smiled at her, got into my car, and reluctantly drove away, wishing I could have caught them that day and not have to come back the next.

"Marcy, I need help!" I said to my Heather Locklear-lookalike rescue friend that night. She agreed to meet me in South Central the next day and brought her friend, Joan Scoccimarro from Adopt A Chow LA. When we got there the puppies were out on the front lawn eating. We waited from a distance for hours, until they had wandered back behind the house, and then made our move. For the rest of the day we boarded up the fences with junk from the yard, while the puppies looked on from under an old car. It's amazing what I have found on people's properties to cover holes and block areas where dogs could escape. This yard was full of things we used, such as empty gas cans, tarps, and wood from the gate that had been torn down. In addition, we had brought a long, tall wrap pen to block the driveway area. By the time we had finished, it was dark, so we moved the food and water into the backyard and secured the wrap pen behind us as we left.

The next morning we came back and spent hours trying to herd the puppies into a corner, where we finally trapped them. The Shepherd mix pup was very sweet and calm once we got him, but the little red bear was like a wild animal, trying with all his might to get out of the loop leash I had put over his head. Once we were able to push him into a crate, he settled down. I will never forget the terrified look on his face as I closed the car door, or how scared he was when we took him out of the crate at the vet.

Driving to South Central that day, I had seen a dog wandering around a park a few blocks away. I went back the next day to discover that he was not the only one there. I then spent the next three months going back and forth, to and from South Central, where I rescued twenty-one dogs in a three-block radius. The majority of dogs had been dumped in the park, where they sat around starving while people walked by without acknowledging them. Most of the dogs were adult Shepherd mixes, older Pit mixes, and puppies of all kinds. I even rescued the little red bear's father—a full-grown replica of the puppy I had by then named Andy.

I spent a large portion of my movie of the week money boarding, vetting, fixing, and microchipping all the dogs. Sadly, I never saw the mother Chow mix, but a young gal adopted Andy's father, who turned out to be the sweetest dog, with no issues. They eventually moved to New York where he became the hit of the Lower East Side. My friend Fred Ponzlov adopted Andy, who adores his dog sister and has grown to trust his human father but is, to this day, wary of anyone else.

I adopted out Andy's brother, Otis, to a wonderful couple, who later had a baby girl. When I checked in recently, after not having spoken to them in a while, here is what they said: "Otis is doing well, considering he gets a fancy raw meat diet, weekly trips to doggie day care, a twice-monthly bath with a bow on the collar when done, teeth cleaning, a Tempur-Pedic mattress, a personal doggie door, free rein of a huge fenced-in backyard, and two walks a day."

During that time, Mary Chapman, another rescuer, called me about a dog chained up in the back of a garage—a huge Ridgeback/Pit mix on a short chain in East LA, where animal abuse and neglect is rampant. *Why is it that the majority of people in some areas have animals and, for the most part, they neglect them?* I wondered as I noticed almost every yard with a lonely dog in it. *Was it for protection?* That seemed unlikely, as the canines I saw were starved for attention and would have allowed anyone on their property. *Or was it lack of education? Did they not understand how animals should be treated?* I understood their working long hours and not having enough money, yet even that would not prevent someone from inviting their dog into the home or taking them on a walk. It broke my heart to see so many animals in need. I wanted to steal them, but where oh where would I put them all?

Marcy and I went by the Ridgeback/Pit's house in the middle of the day, but no one was home. The property had a locked gate around it, so we went back early the next morning and spoke to a man who saw nothing wrong with keeping his dog chained up for the canine's entire life.

I offered him $200 but he declined. I then lied and told him that animal control was going around the neighborhood and fining $1,000 to anyone who had their dog on a chain. He didn't believe me and basically told me to "fuck off." We had some words and Marcy later told me that "I was rude to him and he would never give us the dog now." Was I rude? Absolutely. By that time, I had had it with people abusing and neglecting their animals and had little patience. Being nice was not going to get us the dog anyway.

I knew the laws were not on our side, and in that area, you were *allowed* to chain up a dog, which is horrific—but I had an idea. I called animal control and told them to go out there the next day, knowing the guy would be at work. I told them the dog had no water, which *is* against the law. They went out and left the guy a note saying they were there and for him to contact them (because they could not see the water that was in the back of the garage) and, when the guy came home and got the note, he assumed they had found his dog chained up, and he would be fined the $1,000, like I said. It worked. He called me that evening and asked me to pick up his dog.

We were there the next morning.

I don't know what happened to that Ridgeback/Pit mix, as Mary Chapman, who alerted us, gave him to another rescuer because I had enough to handle. I can only hope his life was better than it was before we got him.

Recently, I was informed that Hank, the biggest, dearest, Pitbull I ever rescued, has cancer. Hank was one of the dogs from South Central.

I had called Animal Control, and they had sent an officer out with a trap to help me get a black Shepherd mix who was running the streets. I had rescued all six of her two-month-old babies, but couldn't get her to trust me. She wouldn't go in the trap, so I drugged her and she went under a house and fell asleep. I crawled after her and almost got a noose around her head, but adrenaline set in when she woke up, and she bolted. The animal control officer chased her. He broke the number one rule. As he pursued her, she ran and ran, and I screamed, "Don't chase her!" It was then I realized that not all animal control officers know what they're doing. I searched for her for days, but sadly, never found her.

When I had shown up at six o'clock the next morning in hopes of finding her in the trap, I saw a huge Pitbull sitting next to it, longing for the chicken inside. He was just too big to get into the trap but had turned it over trying. I slowly got out of my car and approached him, not knowing if he was friendly or not. When I realized he was not a threat, I reached into the trap, got the chicken out, and walked back to my car. He followed me, as I had planned, so I threw the chicken onto the backseat and he jumped in after it. I noticed the cigarette burns on his body, and therefore, didn't even try to search for his owners. After getting him neutered, microchipped, and vetted, I took him to my friend Brian's house. Brian had been fostering a lot of the South Central dogs for me, but he didn't want to keep any of them. On my way there I called him. "You're going to want this one. He looks like he should be your dog," I said.

"Why is that?"

"Because he has a mug on him that reminds me of you. I'm telling you, he's your dog."

Brian did adopt Hank. And years later, the now tripod Pit lives with Brian's ex-girlfriend, Liz, who took Hank after he got his leg removed because of the cancer.

South Central almost did me in, and I never had the "me" time I had hoped for, but it gave me great joy to know all these dogs were rescued, safe, and loved.

CHAPTER ELEVEN

Frankie

"Why are you turning in your dog?" The thirty-something female animal control officer at a shelter in the San Fernando Valley sternly asked the Hispanic boy.

"He's mean. He bites. He's mean." The boy seemed to hesitate before he spoke, but he wanted the officer to know the truth: that if the dog was not mean, he would not be there.

I was at the shelter doing the pull paperwork for two gorgeous Akitas that had been abandoned by a drug dealer. I had possible homes for both of them, and they were going to be sent to the vet to be fixed before I picked them up.

"How old is he?" she asked him.

"Nine-months-old."

I turned around and saw an adorable 35-pound Rottweiler/Cattle Dog mix on a heavy chain, held in the hands of what looked to be the boy's grandfather. I had a feeling the moment the dog was handed over, he would be sent back to the euthanasia room. The shelter was already full of sweet animals that were being put to sleep. A dog relinquished because of biting, no matter how cute, would not be there long.

Though my initial plan was to come later in the day to sign the Akitas out, I had decided to go in the mid-afternoon instead, hoping to miss all the owners dumping their animals after work.

It was this dog's lucky day. Not mine.

Our eyes connected, and he smiled a wide, beautiful smile. I felt like I knew him, like we had met before. He seemed to be saying, "Come to me, you're mine. Stop me from dying before it's too late."

In that instant, I made a pact to myself. *If he tries to bite me, I won't take him.* The dog barked and yelped as he saw me walking toward him.

"No touch," the grandfather said. "Bites."

For some reason, I was not afraid. And he did not bite me. Instead, he jumped up and put his paws around my waist and held on for dear life as I stroked his soft head. His energetic tail thrashed back and forth.

"What is his name?" I asked the grandfather.

"Tyrant," he said.

Oh boy.

The kid walked over. He was very happy that his dog had a woman interested in him.

"What's *your* name?" I asked him.

"Francisco," he said proudly.

"Does he like other dogs? Do you have any other dogs?"

"Yes, yes, he likes dogs. We have another dog and they play."

Tyrant was jumping up and down while still holding onto me. There was no way he was letting me walk out without him.

"Go stand outside with him," I said. "I'll be out in a few minutes."

If I had known what I was getting myself into, I would have kissed the top of Tyrant's head and wished him a good afterlife. At least I would have at *this* juncture in my life, but at *that* point I would have done anything for this dog, and I did.

Once animals are checked into a shelter, you can't just walk out with them. And you're not allowed to relinquish your pet to anyone inside the shelter. You have to be off the premises, which is why I told the boy and his grandfather to go outside.

"You didn't check him in fully, so I'm taking him, okay?" I said to the animal control officer.

"Okay . . . He's all yours," she said sarcastically. They didn't need to kill another dog that day.

I called my dear friends and fellow rescuers, Steve Spiro and Suzanna Urszuly. I had originally met Steve outside a coffee shop when I noticed he and his friend were holding two skinny Pitbulls, who looked like they had just been rescued. Steve is a British writer/actor; Suzanna, a model and a sweetheart. I knew they had room for a foster dog. Within a half hour, Tyrant, who I had re-named Frankie (after Francisco), was playing with their dogs Moi Moi, Marlow, and Ruby.

"They said he bites, but I haven't seen any sign of it yet," I said, as Frankie jumped up and down and kissed them both.

"Our cleaning lady is coming tomorrow, so we'll crate him while she's here, just in case," Suzanna assured me.

"Not to worry, I'm going to bring him in tomorrow to be neutered and chipped," I said.

Suzanna and Steve had previously agreed to take in another dog in need, so Frankie had to move within the week. My friend and facial expert, Myrna Kaufman, who sometimes fostered for me, agreed to take him, even after I told her that he might bite. Myrna was one of the reasons my skin had cleared up from the bad case of acne I'd had many years before, and she was a big animal lover. Her son had passed away a few years earlier, and her daughter-in-law was living with her, but Frankie did not bite either of them, and he loved their dogs.

Where and when is this dog mean? I wondered.

It did not take much longer to find out. A few weeks later, I got a call.

"Well, now I know what they meant," Myrna said. "He has another side to him. I don't think he likes Hispanic women. He attacked my cleaning lady from behind, and thank God I was right there to pull him off her or he would have really hurt her."

"Oh my god! What happened?" I was terribly upset, to say the least.

"She just came in and he went for her. Maybe the Latina mother of the people who had him hurt him, because he wanted to kill her."

I realized by now that he had made himself at home at Myrna's and he was protecting his territory—it had nothing to do with the woman being a Latina. But to *attack* someone?

"Wow, that's scary! Is she okay?" I was appalled.

"Yes, but I'm going to need a crate to put him in when people come over. I can't take a chance."

After I hung up the phone, the words of the Hispanic boy came back to me: "He bites. He's mean. He bites." This was not good.

Over the next few months I tested Frankie, slowly, in different situations, with a muzzle on. At the dog park, Frankie was great with everyone. At adoption events he was fine. But once you came into his home, he would strike. Not just Hispanic women, but mostly everyone.

The day I had taken Frankie from the shelter I had asked Francisco for his phone number, just in case I had any questions about Frankie's upbringing. Well, I now had a big question. What the hell had happened to this dog, and why was he so damaged and dangerous?

Myrna and I came up with different scenarios about what could have made him so fearful and willing to attack someone. He had to have been teased or tormented in some way. Frankie was the smartest, most loyal, loving dog I had ever met. Something *must* have happened to make him like this. But after three days of leaving voice messages, I never found out. Francisco never called me back.

One day at adoptions, a single woman fell in love with my biting rescue dog. She was, she claimed, dog savvy and took her previous canine to work with her. I explained Frankie's behavior in full, but she was not deterred. After a home check, I left Frankie with her. That night I got a phone call.

"Sylva, I have to bring him back to his foster home. He bit my neighbor. I see what you mean now."

I was exasperated. "What do you mean he bit your neighbor? Did she come into your apartment?" I had told this woman over and over again not to let anyone in her apartment without crating Frankie or putting him in another room, and she had made it clear to me that she understood. Now this!

"Well, yes. I guess, I really wanted to see what he would do. I really didn't think he would bite her. He's so sweet. It wasn't bad. I was right there."

"Well just know that it wasn't Frankie's fault. I warned you." What I really wanted to say was, "*You idiot!*" I was pissed and upset at Frankie, the woman, and myself. Back to Myrna's he went, but what the hell was I ultimately going to do with him?

I always nickname dogs, and because Frankie's butt swayed when he walked, I called him Booty. Booty was now showing his real colors.

Shortly thereafter I got a call from Myrna. "Hi, Sylva. I don't know how to tell you this, but we may be sued because Frankie bit a woman." Myrna's friend was housesitting and had agreed to walk Frankie, so I had gone over all the rules, the most important being not to walk him near people. He claimed he understood. Evidently he didn't. The odd thing is, Frankie never bit Myrna's friend, who had walked into Myrna's house like he owned the place that first day, and Booty was in his lap within the hour. It was becoming obvious that this dog did not like it when people showed fear.

Luckily, the woman who Frankie bit dropped the case a few months later when her hand healed, and she realized she had not been hurt that badly.

By now, the situation was really stressing me out. I could not find Frankie a home, as no one wanted a biting dog. I was juggling our household, shooting a guest star appearance on *Cold Case*, and right after that, one of the last episodes of *ER*. Plus driving forty minutes each way, almost every day to Myrna's house, to walk Frankie and her dog—a lovely, female Doberman named Alex. Frankie without exercise would have been even more of a problem. He was a Cattle Dog mix and had lots of puppy energy. He had already eaten Myrna's wicker furniture and put a hole in her Jacuzzi top, both of which I replaced.

As I sat in the makeup trailer getting my hair and makeup done for one of the shows, it dawned on me that my life was a whirlwind of extremes. One minute I was involved with dogs and the underbelly of life and the next I was working in Hollywood and being catered to. It made me think of my mother and how she taught us to treat everyone the same, from the president to the homeless man and how our lives growing up had been varied as well. In the early years she had struggled to pay the rent, and later, after she had re-married, we had lovely homes and traveled around the world. My journey had always been about experiencing the extremes of life, and it was no different now.

Myrna didn't need the drama of Frankie either, as she was in her seventies and had just had heart surgery. Furthermore, with people in and out of her guest house for skin treatments, she had to be very careful to lock him in the main house. God forbid he should bite one of her clients. Myrna was a good sport about it all because she loved animals as much as I did, but this was becoming too much for all of us.

One day, while Frankie and I were at the dog park (where I knew he wouldn't bite anyone because it was neutral territory and he loved to play with his canine friends), animal control was there to pick up two dogs who had been dumped. They looked to be father and son Rottweiler/Shepherd mixes who were sweet, but terrified. I had to leave before the dogs were caught, but later that day I called the shelter to see how they were.

"They're in the back and about to be put down," the officer told me. "They're not friendly at all."

I remembered the look in the eye of the father dog as he was being cornered. It was a look I knew well. A look that said, *I don't know you, and I'm terrified. I've only lived in a backyard all my life and don't know what I'm doing here.*

"They're really sweet dogs. I watched them at the park, and they're just scared."

"Well, whatever. They're going down soon," the impatient officer informed me.

"Actually, I'll be pulling them. Can we do the paperwork over the phone?" I said quickly, before I could talk myself out of it.

My friend, actor Bruno Kirby, had passed away a few months before, and his father, Bruce, was a dear friend as well, so I named the boys Bruce and Bruno. If Frankie and I had not been there that day they would now be dead, but because of Frankie, Bruce and Bruno are now in loving homes. As it turned out, they *were* great dogs!

It was around this time that I decided to remove Frankie's canines, the long, fang-like teeth on each side of his mouth. I spoke to a few trainers and vets and got mixed opinions of whether I should or not. Some told me to just put him down, rather than take his teeth out. But that was not an option for me. Frankie did not have to kill to eat, so he really didn't need his sharp fangs. I knew it could be done rather easily with not a lot of pain for the dog, and knowing how much damage he could cause, I felt it was the right thing for everyone, including myself. After all, I was the one who would be sued if he really hurt anyone. Myrna was not thrilled with the idea, but I did it anyway. Within twenty-four hours, he was back to chewing up her house and playing like the rambunctious puppy he was. He didn't miss a beat.

"Myrna, I have an idea. You know that show with the British dog trainer who goes to people's houses and fixes the dog's behavior? I'm going to see if we can get Frankie on there. She can help him. People will see him and want to adopt him after he's trained." I had hired three trainers for Frankie, and all of them had said the same thing: "Just crate him when people come over." That would have been fine if he had been in his forever home, but finding one with this behavior was nearly impossible.

I called the show, filled out the application, and told them how great it would be to have a rescue dog on there, especially if it helped him find a home. Two weeks later they came to Myrna's house to audition Frankie. As we stood outside, the producer and cameraman were commenting on how cute Frankie was, while I held the leash and explained his behavior to the camera. "Wait until you get in the house. You'll have a whole different opinion of him," I said, before I took Frankie inside.

"Are you ready to come in?" Myrna called to them. I was standing in the corner of the living room with Frankie on leash, while he sat next to me. The plan was for Myrna to greet them as they entered her house, and I would allow Frankie to behave any way he saw fit, while holding the leash so he could not actually get to them.

"Ready!" they called out.

"Oh, do come in," Myrna said in her best hostess voice as she opened the door. They stepped inside and all hell broke loose in Frankie's mind. My sweet, loving, affectionate boy turned into a mad dog—ferocious, baring his teeth, lunging, and screaming at the top of his lungs. He didn't just want to *bite* them. He wanted to *kill* them. I had only been told about this behavior but had never before witnessed it. It made me want to weep for this special dog who was filled with so much fear.

"You get it? Did you get it?" The producer asked the cameraman, with a look of disbelief on her face.

"Yeah, I got it. Wow! That's amazing! He's a totally different dog than the one outside," the cameraman said sadly.

I didn't want Frankie to think what he was doing was okay, so I put him in a down-stay position, got over him and told him, "No!" I was shaking. His behavior was appalling. Worse than I had imagined.

"See what I mean?" Myrna said, with tears in her eyes.

"How soon will we know if he's picked?" I asked in a pleading, pathetic voice.

"By next week. We'll have a meeting and let you know by next week."

The week went by and I didn't hear from them. Two weeks went by. I called them. "Sorry, Sylva, they didn't feel he was a candidate for the show," the secretary said.

"Why, because the trainer didn't think she could work with him? Help him?" I knew the reason was that it was a television show that required a quick fix—and that was not Frankie.

"I'm not sure. He just wasn't picked."

For the first time, I thought of putting a healthy animal to sleep. An old friend of mine had done just that after her dog had bitten three people. At the time I was horrified, but now I was beginning to understand. I couldn't believe I was even toying with the idea, but it was starting to feel like an option. Actually doing it was another thing.

I discussed the possibility with Myrna. She cried and wouldn't hear of it. In all honesty, I would not have been able to do it to Frankie. I was in love with this dog and he with me.

Frankie was adorable, sly, charismatic, funny, loving, very smart, and loyal. But he also had a dark side, and it was scary. If it weren't for the fact that he was a biter, he would have been the greatest dog I ever rescued. Everyone loved him. At least everyone who *he* loved.

I decided I would try to desensitize him to strangers coming into his territory. I tested Frankie with a few more people in Myrna's house: my husband and my dear friend, Amy. They sat in awe as Frankie lunged and growled while I worked with him on the leash and tried to calm him down. Then I decided to test how he would react to someone he'd already met, a person he had learned to love, if only for a few days.

I called Suzanna and asked her to come over. The next day, as I stood in the corner with Frankie on leash, she entered the house. "Hi, Frankie," Suzanna said in her sweet Hungarian accent. "How are you, Frankie?" And with that, Booty was pulling me to get to her. But it was different this time and I knew it immediately. He didn't want to kill her, he wanted to jump up and kiss her, which he did. It was a great experiment because it made me see that Frankie remembered those who were good to him, but it didn't really help me know what to do next.

A year and a half went by since I saved him, and Frankie was now a little over two-years-old and about 45-pounds. In the meantime, Myrna had rescued a Cocker Spaniel from the streets who was more her speed. As much as she loved Booty, she did not want to keep him. I had heard about a trainer who could turn Frankie around, but it would cost me $5,000 for two months, and he would stay at the trainer's house. Jude and I talked about it, and my dear husband, though reluctant, agreed to pay for it. He had seen the stress and struggle I had dealt with having taken on this biting dog, and he wanted to be the one to help me—and Frankie.

A week after Booty went to the trainer, my Beauty Princess, my Sammy, my soulmate girl, suddenly got ill. She had been moving very slowly on our walks, something she did occasionally, to let me know she was in control.

"Come on, my Princess, knock it off," I would say, as I tugged on her to let her know who was boss. She was strong-willed, just like her mama. We sometimes quarreled, like mother and daughter, but we loved each other fully and completely.

Jude and I called her Ellery Princess, after the detective Ellery Queen, because she wanted to know and be involved in everything. My grandmother had married one of the writers of the Ellery Queen mystery stories when my mom was a kid, and he was the only grandfather I knew on my mother's side.

But the walk that day was different and within twenty-four hours, Sammy had stopped eating. I took her to the vet and after the X-rays showed nothing wrong, they gave her some antibiotics, thinking she had a stomach flu or something. She didn't eat for two days. Then, Friday evening, I walked into our bedroom, and she was not in her usual place—on our bed. I found her outside, lying on one of the red-and-orange-striped dog beds. The sun was setting behind her, bouncing off her beautiful strawberry blonde fur and casting a glow around her and the colorful, comfortable bed. "My Princess, are you okay? Why are you outside? Do you want to come in? Mama take you back to the vet tomorrow." Sammy got up and walked very slowly toward me. She had that sick, old dog look, which had happened overnight. Her body was weak, her movement slow and uneasy. She looked at me with her brown, soulful eyes, and it was then that I noticed her nose was bleeding—a lot! "Oh my god, sweetheart, we have to get you to the vet, right now," I said. But what I really thought was, *We have to put you out of your misery.* I would not let *her* suffer. Not after what Charlie had gone through.

Jude was shooting an episode of *The Mentalist,* so I left him a message saying I was taking Sammy to the vet and to meet me there. He called back immediately and told me to wait for him. "Hurry," I said. "I can't wait that long." It was after six p.m., so I took her to the 24-hour emergency. Within an hour, Jude was there.

"We can run some tests if you want," the female vet suggested.

"No, thank you. My daugh . . . my dog is dying. I don't need a test to tell me that. I don't want her to suffer, but thank you anyway." I was on autopilot. A mix of emotions propelled me to make the hardest decision of my life. One part of my mind was screaming at me to do anything to save my ten-year-old dog; the other part knew it was too late and wanted her to be at peace. We held our girl and told her how much we loved her while her tail thumped hard (like it did every time we approached her) against the soft blanket she was lying on. The vet administered an I.V. injection to relax her. Once Sammy seemed comfortable, she gave her a second injection to stop her heart, and the life went out of our beloved dog's eyes as she slipped away. I sobbed from the bottom of my soul, as if I had just lost a child, which I had—a four-legged one. And I wondered if I had done the right thing.

We brought her body home so that Mazie and Beau Bo could say goodbye. The next morning, Jude and I took her to be cremated, which was very hard for me. I did not want to let my girl go. I held her and stroked her stiff body. To me, she was still there. "I love you, my Beauty Princess," I said as I clung to her before they wheeled her away. "Thank you for being my Princess. Mama love you. I will always love you."

And then she was gone. My Sammy was gone.

The timing was uncanny—as if she were making room for Frankie to be able to live with us. As if she were trying to help me out, so I didn't have to go through any more drama, finding the biting dog a home.

I love all my dogs and all the dogs I have rescued, but my Princess was my first and she was a part of me. We were one. We still are. I wish all animals could be loved and appreciated like Sammy was. I sometimes wonder: *Where is she? How could she not be here? Where is my Princess?*

Hopefully, one day I will see her again standing at the Rainbow Bridge, where dogs are supposed to be waiting for their loved ones as they cross over. When she realizes it's me, her ears will be up and alert, her eyes focused, and her head cocked to one side and then another. As I walk toward her, her big, beautiful smile will spread across her wise, gorgeous face. She will take off running toward me, throw herself into my open arms, and we will be together once again.

We decided to bring Frankie home after the training and make him ours. But even after Jude went with me to the trainer's to see our new dog every week and Frankie knew Jude, he still tried to bite him the night we brought him home. He was *very* bonded to me, intent on protecting me in our house.

As Jude describes it, what had happened was my husband went to get Frankie out of his training crate that first morning, and it was as if Frankie had turned into Lon Chaney Jr. as the Wolfman, baring his teeth and threatening to bite.

$5,000 down the drain.

I could not keep this dog. I decided I was going to put him down, or at least I was talking about it again, but Jude wouldn't let me. "There has to be some solution for him," he said. "And I just paid $5,000!"

I took Frankie to see Myrna and her dogs the week I got him back, thinking he would be so happy to have a play date with Alex and see his foster mama. But the strangest thing happened. It was the oddest canine behavior I have ever witnessed. Every time a dog is rescued and brought back to the place they were first loved, they are happy as hell to see the person who took care of them when they most needed it. That was not the case this time. You would have thought this dog had never met Myrna or been to her house.

Frankie got out of my car and instead of doing his booty dance and running up to kiss the woman who took care of him for almost two years, he walked around, smelled her front yard, and ignored her. He wouldn't even look at Myrna. For a moment, I was afraid he was going to bite her.

When we brought him through the side gate into her backyard, Alex came bounding out through the doggy door to see him. But he only gave his old friend a brief show of recognition, then came over to me and sat down. It was bizarre. Myrna was crushed. I was shocked.

"Frankie, what's going on?" I asked him, but he walked over to the gate, letting me know it was time to go. It broke my heart because I knew that this highly intelligent dog remembered Myrna, and Alex, and his old home. That was not the problem. The problem was that he felt like this family, his first loving family, had abandoned him. And now that he was my dog, he no longer wanted anything to do with them. That's how aware and sensitive he was.

Over the next few days, Myrna and I dissected Frankie's behavior, and I assured her it was not because Booty didn't care about them. Quite the opposite. He had loved them very much.

The thing is, Frankie was not just a dog to me. He reminded me of someone from my past who I had once loved very much, but had caused me a lot of pain. Rather, I had caused myself a lot of pain, because of him. His name was Scott.

There had been an instant attraction and coming together when Scott and I met. It was like we had known each other in a past life. We were in each other's lives, one way or another, until the week he died of alcoholism sixteen years later. I was married by then, but I and a few others, including his siblings, took care of his belongings and made sure his three beloved dogs all found a new home together. He had been a terrific actor but he was a tortured soul, and I felt that Frankie was Scott reincarnated. I had saved Booty the week of Scott's birthday. Both had similar personality traits: loving to some, cruel to others. Both were good-looking, smart, sly, charismatic, and tormented. And one of Scott's beloved dogs had been named Frankie.

I had one more person to reach out to, to save *this* Frankie—one last hope. I had not talked to him in a few years.

"Hi, Robin, this is going to sound very strange, but I rescued a dog that I believe is Scott reincarnated, and I think he's supposed to be with *you*." I felt that all the drama I was going through with this animal was because I was meant to bring him to Robin, Scott's best male friend, the person he had loved more than anyone at the time of his death.

Robin resided in Montana with his girlfriend, Nancy, along with four cats, and four dogs. Their beautiful house was on eleven acres. The dogs went hiking every day and lived inside as family. This was a perfect home for any animal—or person, for that matter.

"I'm not making this up. I have come to believe that this dog has Scott's soul, and I'm going to have to put him to sleep unless you take him." It was not a threat, just the truth.

"Well, that's odd, because I thought *we* had Scott here."

"What do you mean?" I asked.

"I think I told you that the day after Scott died, this little kitten showed up in our driveway out of nowhere." They lived in the middle of nowhere—beautiful, peaceful nowhere. "Remember when Scott the kitten was really sick and became addicted to pain medication?"

I laughed. "Yes, I do remember that, now. How apropos for Scott. But I'm telling you, this is Scott too. Maybe a little of his soul is in each of these animals?"

After I told Robin and Nancy the whole story, they agreed that if Frankie was good with their cats and dogs, they would take him. "We have insurance," Robin said. "I'm not worried about him biting anyone."

I tested Frankie the next day with a cat who belonged to a friend of mine, and he had no reaction at all. Yay! One hurdle down.

That Friday, at six a.m., Jude drove Frankie and me, along with Charlie's flying crate, to the Burbank airport. The plan was for me to bring Frankie to Montana and stay a few days. If it worked out, I would leave him there. If it didn't . . . I only had one other choice.

"Sorry, but the weather in Montana is too cold today, so you won't be able to fly," the woman behind the counter informed me.

"You've gotta be kidding me." I stared at her with my mouth open.

"No, it's too cold. You can try tomorrow when the temperature is supposed to be warmer."

My husband does not do well with plans changing. "Unbelievable! I can't believe this!" he exclaimed.

"Well, believe it. It's happening," I said, trying to calm myself down as well.

"What if tomorrow is the same thing, what if . . ."

"Relax honey. We'll get there. One way or another, we'll get there," I assured us both.

The next morning there we were, the three of us, back at the airport. An airport employee wanted to take Frankie out of the crate to frisk him. "Unless you want your hand bitten off, I wouldn't do that," I informed her. "I'll frisk him for you." The employee understood and watched as I took Booty out of the crate and showed her that there was nothing illegal or harmful in the crate or on his body. I had given him a tranquilizer for the trip, so he was more agreeable than usual.

When we arrived at Robin and Nancy's house, all their dogs came out to greet him, one at a time, which I knew wouldn't be a problem. He trusted all animals, just not all humans. Montana was beautiful; there was still snow on the ground. The air was crisp and clear, and Frankie ran around their property like the free, alive dog he was. The others ran with him and invited Booty into their pack.

Robin and Nancy's home was built to look like a large, old mountain cabin. Their animals lounged freely and comfortably wherever they wanted. I was not worried about Frankie biting either of them, because we were on *their* property and in *their* home.

If I had any doubt that Booty was meant to be with Robin, it was washed away when Frankie ran up the stairs to chase one of their cats that first night as we were sitting down for Nancy's delicious dinner. Robin jumped up and swatted him on the bottom. I held my breath, waiting for Frankie to turn and attack him, but he didn't. Booty was home and he knew it.

Nancy was a Cesar Millan (the guru dog trainer) follower, so she was looking forward to working with Frankie, and she set about it right away on their walks. He was in good hands. She was loving but firm, which gave him a feeling of trust and security.

I sobbed the night I said goodbye and held him at the bottom of their guest room stairs. "Don't screw this up. You have a chance for a great life, and there's nothing else I can do, as much as that breaks my heart," I told him. "I love you, Booty, and I always will. You be a good boy. I love you." I held his face and kissed him. He licked the tears that were streaming down my cheeks and looked into my eyes. I then pulled myself together and walked back into the kitchen. "Just remember," I said to Robin and Nancy. "Muzzle or crate him when guests come over."

Almost a month later, the phone rang as I was about to walk out the door. The woman on the other end was sobbing. "Who is this?" I said, trying to understand what she was saying.

"It's Nancy," she cried. "Frankie attacked our friend from behind. It was awful."

My heart stopped. *Thank God his canines were removed.*

"How bad did he bite him?"

"The act was scarier than the actual bite, but he really attacked him."

I had warned them.

After we calmed down, Nancy and I agreed that Frankie should be put to sleep. But she didn't want to be the one, and the thought of flying back to Montana to do it gave *me* a severe head and heartache.

Luckily, Robin wouldn't hear of it. "He'll get better. Now we know. We won't let it happen again," he assured me.

They had to see it firsthand. I told them what could happen, but they had to see it. Now they knew what they were dealing with.

It's been over four years since Frankie went to live with Robin and Nancy, and I couldn't be more grateful that they took him. Booty is living his happy Montana life, and his behavior *has* gotten better.

Reimbursing Myrna, gas driving back and forth to walk him, teeth removal, training, and a plane flight cost Jude and me almost $10,000. Was he worth it? Yes. Would I ever invest so much time, money, and energy in another biting dog? No . . . Never again.

One day I plan on going back to Montana. I look forward to spending some time with Frankie in his later years and seeing how the fearful puppy I rescued has grown into a trusting old dog, in the hands of Robin and Nancy.

One day I will do that. I think that will make Frankie—and me— very happy.

CHAPTER TWELVE

Thank God for Jude

If it weren't for my husband, I would not have become an animal rescuer, at least not to the extent that I am today. When Jude and I married, he let me know that he would pay the house bills and that I did not have to worry about monthly expenses. My husband was making a lot more than I was, so the money I earned was spent to pay my personal bills as well as any other way I saw fit, which, later on, was to rescue animals.

People have always asked me why? Why do I rescue dogs?

I rescue dogs because I can.

I rescue dogs because they need to be rescued.

I rescue dogs because I know what it's like to be in pain in this world, and when I see someone, person or animal, in need, I help.

But there is another reason I rescue dogs—the beginning, middle, and end. I am, I believe, addicted to transformation in all areas of my life. I have spent time on bettering myself, and I see the results. I work on a character as an actor, I see the results. I decorate a house, I see the results. I write a book, I see the results. I rescue a dog, I see the results. (I rescue, care for, and place in a forever home—there's a beginning, middle, and end). And by doing so, there is one less animal in the world to worry about. Yet there is an even more important reason: Nothing is as rewarding as seeing a soul in need and, with some intervention, seeing them happy and at peace. Really, there is nothing better. And knowing that you have the power to make that happen is amazing.

On the flip side, the reason I hate rescue work is that it's never done. For every dog I save, millions and millions are still suffering. That's why rescue work is so difficult, especially for someone like me. In the big picture, I know that I will never see the end result I wish for.

A question I get asked frequently is: "How do you do it? How can you bond to these dogs and then adopt them out?"

"It's easy," I say. "I'm the vessel they pass through to get to their rightful home. If I brought them to my house and kept all of them, I would be a divorced hoarder, with no other life." There were some animals I wish I could have kept. A few dogs that touched me deeply; beautiful, soulful creatures that I felt were meant to be mine. But alas, they are not and never will be.

Another question I get asked is: "What does your husband think of all this? All the time and money you've spent rescuing dogs. What does he think?"

"He thinks I'm a hero," I reply. "That I'm Saint Francis." But he also thought I shouldn't be as immersed in rescue as I was. "Stop!" I heard him say through the years. "Give yourself a break." It worried him that I had gotten so wrapped up and stressed over feeling like I could save the world and, quite frankly, it started to worry me too. At first, I thought I *could* save the world, or at least a portion of it around me. But there came a time when I had to make a choice and save myself. "*Dogs have to die, so you can live,*" I told myself.

I remember lying in bed one morning feeling paralyzed, absolutely unable to move. My thoughts went something like this: *If I get up, I'm going to have to listen to my message machine and hear that Leo is not getting along with their dog, that they want to give him back, and I have nowhere for him to go. Then I'm going to hear two more messages about someone wanting to give up their dogs and then one of yet another dog being returned. When I check my e-mail, I'm going to see at least fifty dogs that are being put to sleep and other e-mails about dogs on their way to the shelter or on the streets that need to be rescued.*

It seemed like all my awake time was spent worrying about an animal situation. When I got an audition and then a job, I relished being in someone else's head. I immersed myself completely, which was great for my sanity and my work. Having the balance of both the acting and rescue worlds in my life was a good thing at first, until the rescue world started to take over and I thought I would have a nervous breakdown.

One balmy August evening in 2008, as I rushed from my car into the emergency room at St. Joseph's Hospital in Burbank, I was amazed that the waiting area was almost empty. "Hi, I'm having heart palpitations and I need to be seen by a doctor," I said. After I filled out the paperwork, which took so long I could have had a heart attack right there and then, I was escorted into a room where a young attendant hooked me up to a machine.

"Yeah, your heart is not beating right. It's definitely abnormal. Are you stressed?"

A strange, high-pitched giggle came from somewhere deep inside of me. "Stressed? Stressed? Yes, I *am* stressed . . . *very* stressed!"

After an hour, my heart was beating back to normal, and I was released with the suggestion to be *less* stressed.

The next day, I went to my husband's heart doctor. For twenty-four hours, I had to wear a monitor, which determined that I had a slight arrhythmia, an irregular heartbeat. "Nothing to really worry about," the doctor said. "Just simplify your life, so you're not so *stressed.*"

"If it were only that easy," I thought.

Luckily, I have always worked out every day, which helped me and my stress, but the key was to find some peace of mind. I knew that would never happen if I kept myself tightly involved with the rescue community and continued receiving emails every day about animals in need. So I made a decision. I would take myself off the email blasts, and I would not pull any more dogs from death row. Nor would I give my number out to everyone who might one day need help placing their animal in another home. The only dogs I would rescue were ones that were put directly in my path, such as a dog on the street or a friend needing help with a situation. That way I could de-stress and concentrate more on taking care of myself. And it worked. For a few months. Until the day I walked into Pet Mania, only to face the biggest rescue challenge of my life.

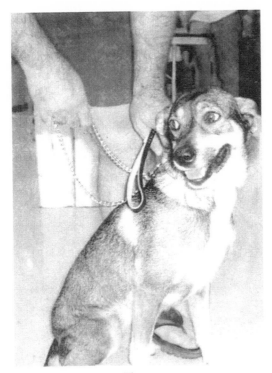

Trixie

Suzanne & Scarlett

Samantha

Andy the little red bear

Otis & Family

Hank & Liz

Frankie

Nancy & Robin

Jude & I on our way to the Sag Awards

CHAPTER THIRTEEN

The Landfill

Just when I thought I was out, they pull me back in.

I can remember the day, just as I remember the above line from *The Godfather: Part 3*. It was the end of summer, when one can feel the heavy heat in the air start to dissipate, and the Santa Ana winds blow the smog out of the Valley so the clouds can be seen.

I was at Pet Mania dropping off a dog who I had taken to adoptions. He had been returned the week before because he was destructive, and the people didn't want to deal with it. I had placed him, so I felt responsible and wanted to find him the *right* home where he could get the proper training for his behavior. If I had walked out the door one minute sooner, Laura, the manager, who had become my friend, would have told the caller she couldn't help and to contact a rescue group. But I was there. One more minute, and I would have been gone. "Sylva, there's a woman on the line who wants help with a mama and pup in Sun Valley. Can you talk to her?"

"You know I'm trying not to rescue anymore," I said. "You don't have room to take any dogs in, so you know I'm going to be stuck helping her." Laura gave me a quick glance, put the phone on the counter, and turned to help a waiting customer. "Thanks a lot." I glared at her back. *Sun Valley. Where Scarlett lives.* "Hello, can I help you?" I said impatiently, as I held the phone to my ear.

"Yes, I live in Sun Valley, and I saw a mother dog and her puppy run under a fence near the landfill. I don't know what to do. If I call animal control, they will take them and put them to sleep.

"What kind of dog?" I asked.

"Maybe some kind of Pit mix? She was small and brown and—"

"If I get the dogs, can you take them?"

"Well, I really don't have room for . . ." Her words trailed into a familiar silence.

I was so used to these kinds of calls by now, people who wanted to help animals, but only as much as their comfort zone allowed, which generally wasn't very much. "Where is the landfill? Give me an exact address. If I get the dogs, can you contribute to their vet and boarding expenses?" I asked her.

"I really don't have—"

"Okay, just give me the address."

The next day I drove out to the landfill in Sun Valley to find what I thought would be just a mama and her pup. So as not to scare them, I parked a hundred feet away from the side of the fence, where I was told the dogs were going in and out. As I walked toward the area where they were seen, I noticed a huge bowl of food and another bowl of water under the fence. *That's a lot of food for two dogs,* I thought. I slowly crept up to the fence and peered in, but I quickly realized that I was the one being watched. At least forty pairs of eyes stared back at me. It was then that I wondered, *Do I save these dogs, or do I save myself?*

In the next instant, what I saw made my jaw drop: there, emblazoned on the green tarp covering the fence, were the letters "SK." My initials. *My god, why me and how?* I wanted and needed so badly to spend energy and time on myself, yet here I was presented with the largest rescue I was ever to experience.

"Ha! Ha!" the tarp seemed to taunt, as it blew in the wind. "You're the one who has to help. It's all up to you!" I wanted to cry. I didn't know if the woman lied, saying there were only two dogs or if that's all she saw, but there were at least forty dogs and puppies on the other side of the fence. I could tell there were more in the landfill by the way some of them scurried up and down the hill.

This was not a landfill for residential trash, but a dump for smashed concrete, dirt, and discarded construction materials. It extended about a half mile in either direction. I looked over the vast emptiness and then scanned down the hill, where the dogs had fled for cover. It was clear that they felt protected below, hiding in the trees and shrubbery at the bottom of the ravine. *So out of place for a landfill, being right in the middle of a residential neighborhood,* I thought. I realized that the area around the makeshift forest, would eventually be filled to the top. *How many more dogs are down there?* I wondered.

That night I lay in my bed, frozen with anxiety and anger. Angry with God for putting me in this position, stressed about how I was going to handle it.

The next day I returned with Simone, the owner of Pet Mania. Our plan was to try to get as many puppies as we could, then talk to the landfill workers about what was going on. Simone had agreed to make room for some puppies but couldn't take any of the adults.

When we arrived, we saw a beat-up old white car. A woman in her seventies with white hair and glasses was kneeling down filling up food bowls. She had on gray sweat pants and a black-and-white patterned jacket that, at one time in the past, she had most likely worn with dress pants and heels. "Hi. I was called to help a stray dog and her puppy, only to find there are many more here. Can you tell me why? By the way, my name is Sylva." I held out my hand and leaned down toward her.

"Hi, I'm June," she said as she tried to get herself up off the ground.

"Please, don't." I knelt down beside her. "What's going on here?"

"I've been feeding them for about eight years," she sighed. "People dump them unfixed, so a lot have been born here."

"How many do you think there are?"

June smiled and giggled like a schoolgirl, in a way I would come to know and love. "Your guess is as good as mine," she said. And then she asked very sweetly, "Do you want one? Is that why you're here?"

"I wish it were that simple," I laughingly informed her.

After I told June how I came to be there, she described some of the dogs' histories. "I've seen so many come and go. Julie around the corner has Diego, and Diego's mother is now in boarding and has been for years."

For years? I was astonished! This was the first time I had ever heard of a dog being boarded for years. Unfortunately, I came to find out that it's a common occurrence, because a lot of "rescue" people pay to keep dogs in boarding facilities instead of trying to find them a forever home.

"Yes, the guy who pulled her out of here also has three that he keeps in his car, day and night, with one of them being kept in a crate."

I was horrified. Especially after she told me that he may have been one of the people dumping dogs as well.

I illegally climbed under the fence to sit with a few of the older dogs who weren't scared of me. The others had run away down the hill. That night Simone and I took two puppies who hadn't yet learned to be too afraid of people. Within the week, I met the manager of the landfill who gave me permission to climb under the fence and retrieve as many dogs as I could.

One evening, as I stood above the landfill, I looked down to see King, as we would come to name him. King was a huge yellow Shepherd mix who seemed to be the alpha male running the pack. As he stopped, I looked to my right to witness the most amazing sight—I saw at least twenty dogs running to greet him. It was beautiful to see all those dogs hail their "king!" As the sun set behind them, I was filled with a feeling of wonder and dread. *What was I going to do with all of these animals?*

Over time, Simone and I made multiple trips to catch more puppies, along with a few of the older, friendly dogs, which we took back to her pet store.

That helped immensely, yet it still left me scrambling to find shelter for close to forty dogs, some of which were feral animals who had never been touched or had direct contact with humans. At least fifteen of the dogs in the landfill had been born on site, and except for seeing the landfill workers at a distance, had never experienced being close to a human.

That year, June and I spent a lot of time together. She had been a starlet in her day and had once been married to David Nelson, the brother of Ricky Nelson. June was a huge animal lover and had discovered the landfill years before while driving to feed some nearby feral cats. Some of the dogs were friendly enough to let me put a loop around their necks as they ate out of my hand, but most of them had to be trapped. The guys at the landfill would set the trap at night, then call me in the morning to let me know if anyone had been captured. When a dog was trapped, I would transport the animal to the vet in the neighborhood to be spayed/neutered, vaccinated, and microchipped. After they had been fixed and vetted, I would either take them to a temporary boarding facility or put them in a foster home until I found them a forever home. This went on for over a year; I was on automatic pilot.

I brought the older, feral dogs, who were black and looked like Shepherd/Lab/Coyote mixes, to a man with a large, secure property. He was willing to take them and had the money for extended care. King, who was not feral, went there as well. He wanted to stay with his buddies. One by one, I found homes for the others: Pit and Shepherd mixes mostly, all colors, all sizes.

I have always had amazing luck placing dogs in wonderful homes. My rescue friends are astounded at the homes I find within a short period of time. Here's my secret I tell them: "I pray. It works."

New dogs would show up at the landfill pretty frequently. On one occasion, it was a purebred Akita who I assumed had been dumped there. She was in heat and sick. I named her June, a.k.a. June Bug, after the woman who had been feeding them. Once June was seen by a vet and started feeling better, I had her spayed, microchipped, and took her to Pet Mania. She stayed there until I found her a great home with a lesbian couple, their Pitbull, and a cat.

Four months later, I got a call from a woman who had seen June Bug's picture on the Akita website, where I had posted her. I'd forgotten to remove the image after she was placed in a home. The caller claimed June was hers and that, months before, she had gotten out of her house. The Akita had not been previously spayed, nor did she have a microchip or identification tags—basically nothing to say that the dog had once had a good home. When I found her, there were only signs of neglect.

The gals refused to give June Bug back, which made me happy. So the caller sued Pet Mania and me for $25,000. "Sylva!" I heard my husband's angry voice on the other end of the line. "You just got served by the court. You're being sued for $25,000. We don't have $25,000 to give this woman over a dog!" He was pissed!

"Honey, relax," I said. "She doesn't have any right to this dog and she knows it. She found out I'm an actress and is just trying to scare me in the hope of getting some money." Which was true. "I'll be home soon." As calm as I sounded, I was freaked out. I had never been sued by anyone, and it scared the hell out of me. The adage "No good deed goes unpunished" came to mind.

Simone and I hired a lawyer and spent $2,500 that could have been used to help animals. After waiting weeks for a mediation or trial date, I suggested my lawyer let the woman suing us know that if she lost the case, I would sue *her* ass off! The next day he called to inform me she was dropping the case. The woman had claimed she loved her dog, but had done nothing to try to find her when she had escaped. She had never put up any flyers in the area, hadn't protected her with an ID tag or microchip, and had never had the dog spayed. I believe she found the picture when she started looking to get another dog. If she had searched the Akita Rescue website four months before when she lost her dog, she would have seen June Bug's picture.

This was not a worthy owner, at least not in my book.

It took almost two years but, little by little, dog by dog, I rescued forty-five canines from that landfill, plus twenty from the surrounding neighborhood. The dogs ranged from Chihuahuas who had been dumped, to various mixes of Shepherds, Pits, and Labs. They included a pure Pitbull with scars all over his face, Tee, a Pit mix with a broken leg that required surgery and took months to heal, and a beautiful Shepherd with her nine babies who I found in a neighborhood car parts junk yard.

When I was done, there were three boys left in the landfill. I had tried everything, but couldn't rescue them. After seeing their siblings and friends caught, they would come nowhere near the trap, which was my only way of catching the feral dogs. I knew they were males when no more babies were born, so I felt safe giving myself a break. Also, by this time, we had closed the hole in the fence bordering the landfill so no other dogs could enter from the main street. If anyone dumped a pet, the dog would have to travel into the neighborhood, but the remaining landfill dogs could still get out to wander the neighborhood from the other side.

June was getting older and had a son she had to care for. To ease her burden every month, I would drop off kibble, and the guys who worked at the landfill kept the food and water bowls filled for the remaining dogs. I felt terrible that I couldn't catch them, but I had to walk away for the time being. There was nothing else I could do.

CHAPTER FOURTEEN

Billy, Millie, and Shadow

By now I was getting back some semblance of my life. I was working on TV and doing some theater, as well as taking the time to have massages and facials-indulgences I love! Plus, I was spending more time with my husband and my own dogs. I was still rescuing, just not as much as before. Now I was hooked up with a woman named Linzi Glass, an author and writing teacher who had gotten into rescue after she fostered some dogs for me. We had not only become friends, but rescue partners as well. It was at this time that she decided to start The Forgotten Dog Foundation, which would help us pay for the animals, as people could donate and get a tax deduction. The Foundation also allowed us to solicit food donations, so we didn't have to pay for dog food, which was a huge help. The plan was for me to be cofounder of the Foundation, but when I realized this would suck me even deeper into the rescue world instead of easing the pressure, I pulled out. I still remained involved, however, as a board member, and working on the periphery.

Around this time I received a call from a woman I had given my number to a few years before. She had been at the dog park with her unfixed Pitbull, and I had explained to her that she should not bring an unfixed dog into the park because other males usually become aggressive toward unfixed males. I also stressed that she simply should not have an unfixed dog. I gave her the number of an inexpensive vet; she got her Pit neutered the following week. "Hi, Sylva. Remember me, Natalia? You told me where to get my dog neutered."

"Yes. Hi, Natalia. What's up?" I said, fully expecting her to tell me she could no longer keep the dog.

"Sylva, my boyfriend lives in an apartment in Compton. His neighbor keeps her Pitbull puppy on the balcony all the time, even in the hot sun, with no water, and never lets him in the house."

Great. "Has he tried talking to her? Asked his neighbor to give the dog up or called animal control?"

"Yeah, but the animal control officer said the puppy had water when they went there, so they were okay with the situation."

I was sick and tired of the laws, which in this country are archaic regarding animals. If the dog has shade and water he/she could be confined to a tiny area his/her whole life. The need for exercise, and the opportunity to move around, or for love, or companionship, are not on the law books—not yet anyway. "The dog has no shade the majority of the day," she said. "Maybe there was shade when they visited, so they said it was okay."

I understood that LA animal shelters were overwhelmed. Officers responding to a call hope they don't have to confiscate another animal. "So who owns the dog? Are they home during the day? Can I get to the balcony without them being there?" I asked.

"No, it's high up," she said. "A young woman and her two kids live there. Her husband is in jail."

The next day, Steve Spiro (my friend who had fostered Frankie the first week) and I were on the 5 Freeway driving to Compton. By now I was used to showing up at people's houses unannounced and questioning them about the care of their dogs, which scared my husband. "Be careful. One day you're going to get yourself killed talking to the wrong guy," he would caution.

I was careful, but I was also fearless when it came to doing the right thing.

"Okay, here's the building," I said, when I saw what looked like a black-and-white Pit/Bulldog on a balcony to our right. "Let's drive around the side and see if there is any way we can get up there." Unfortunately, the property was completely fenced in and gated, so we had to wait for an opportunity. Ten minutes later, someone was driving out, and we were able to enter the complex. Soon we were knocking on the front door. "Hi, we're from an animal rescue group and we got a call about your dog." I couldn't see who was standing on the other side of the metal security screen door. It was the kind where the inhabitants can see out, but you can't see in.

"What about my dog?" a bitchy female voice responded.

"Can we come in?" Steve asked.

"You got a warrant? If you ain't got a warrant, you ain't comin' in."

"Can you open your door so we can talk to you? We just want to help," I calmly assured her.

She cracked the door slightly. "Animal people were here," she informed us. "They said my dog was okay."

"Well, they were wrong, Miss," Steve told her. "Your dog has no shade out there on the balcony. He's a big puppy that needs exercise and shouldn't be kept on a small patio. Do you ever walk him?"

"I used to, but he's too big, and he can knock my kids down. So he's outside, and it's none a' your business."

I stuck my foot in the door before she could close it. "You're so pretty. What's your name?" I said, as I peeked around the door to see her. She was a very pretty Hispanic gal, no more than twenty-three.

"Mary," she said warily, but I could see the slight smile creep along the side of her mouth.

"Well, Mary, I know you have your hands full with kids, and you don't need a big Pitbull who is growing larger every day on your patio. We help dogs get wonderful homes, and we'd like to take yours off your patio and get him a home where he can run free and live with other dogs and people. I know you care about him and want what's best for him. If he stays, you're going to have to get him licensed, neutered, and get his shots. All that costs *a lot* of money. Plus, your neighbors are complaining about him being there, so why don't you do the right thing? You seem like a really good person who could use a break. We'll be more than happy to help you and get your dog the right home." After another fifteen minutes of cajoling, kissing her ass, and explaining to her what an animal needs, she agreed to talk to her husband when she visited him in jail the next day.

As Steve and I headed back to my car, a man who had overheard our conversation stopped us. "Hey, you animal people? I got a complaint. My neighbor lets her dogs bark."

"I don't let my dogs bark. You're the one trying to poison my dogs! He's trying to poison my dogs!" a woman screamed from behind him.

"It's all yours," I said to my rescue friend, and as I stood back to watch Steve mediate, I had to laugh. Our lives were like a one-hour drama. By the time we left, the neighbors had agreed to get along and not threaten each other.

The next day I got a call from Mary. "Hi, Sylva. Okay, you can have him."

"I know a woman who wants to foster a male Pit," Steve's wife, Suzanna, said. "She lives in Sun Valley. Her name is Lisa Chiarelli."

I had not been on the landfill street for almost a year. When I arrived with food, I always brought it to the office, which was a few blocks away. And now I found myself sitting in front of Lisa's house on the street where I had rescued so many dogs. "I can't believe you live here. I know your street very well," I said to her, as I untied Billy (the balcony dog's new name) from my car. "How bizarre that you live here. I rescued dogs right here for years."

"Wow, that's amazing. I've never seen any dogs here, but I've only been here about a year."

As we took Billy and Lola, Lisa's Pitbull, for a walk down the street that I had spent so much time on, I told Lisa all about my landfill experience. I noticed that the initials SK, now faded, were still on the green tarp, and it made me sad that I hadn't gotten all the dogs out of there.

The next day Lisa called: "Okay, you know how you told me that you rescued so many dogs from the landfill and from my street, and I told you I had never seen a dog loose around here before . . . well, I did this morning. There, on my street, was a really mangy looking Pitbull mix being humped by a purebred Shepherd, who was taking turns along with what looked like a black Shepherd mix."

I took a deep breath. *Here we go again.* "Well, I think the black dog is from the landfill," I said. "Is he about 55-pounds with short hair and big ears?" At least twenty of the landfill dogs had looked like that; presumably all came from the same lineage. A coyote must have mated with one of the original black Lab/Shepherds who was dumped there.

"Yes, and the Pitbull-looking female has a wire tied around her neck," Lisa informed me. "And she has the worst case of mange I've ever seen on a dog."

"Where are they now?" I asked.

"I don't know. I had to leave for work, but I'll look when I get back." That evening Lisa called me again. "Okay, when I was coming up Sunland Boulevard"—which was a few blocks away from her house—"the three of them were on the side of the road humping, with the traffic whizzing close by. They're going to get themselves killed!"

"I'm sure that's the last thing they're thinking about," I quipped.

The next morning I went out to see if I could easily capture the other two dogs who had evidently been left there. As I drove around the neighborhood, I thought how ironic it was that I had been brought back here at this particular time. Lisa had not seen any dogs in a year. Now, a day after I meet her, she sees three.

"Hi," I called to the worker who had pulled into the rental truck company across the street from the landfill. "I'm looking for some dogs. Have you seen any dogs running loose in the last few days?"

The young, dark-haired man looked me up and down. "Why? You lost your dogs?"

"No, I'm trying to rescue some dogs that were dumped around here. Have you seen them?"

"Yeah, I've seen them; they're around here somewhere. They've been here for a few days. They hide under the trucks at the other end, but you can't go back there. It's against our policy."

"Then who do I have to talk to?"

A smile spread across his face as he realized I was not going away. "Me, you can talk to me," he said.

"Okay then, I'm talking to you and I'm asking you if I can go back there, because I need to rescue the dogs. Okay?"

He took a moment before responding. I could see the wheels turning. "Okay, but be careful you don't get run over or anything. Insurance, you know."

I looked around the rental lot. Not a truck was moving in either direction. "I'm sure I'll be fine. Thanks."

The young man leaned against his car as he watched me walk into the lot. I knew what he was probably thinking; it's what most people think when I show up to rescue dogs: *Why? Why does she care so much about a dog?*

There was a time when I would have been horrified to be thought of as a dog rescuer. But those days are over. Other people's opinions of me no longer matter in that regard. Whatever people think about my trying to help dogs in need is not my concern.

I immediately knew where they were when I entered the lot. There was a large truck at the far end and I could see some shadows under it. As I got closer, I crouched down and witnessed one of the most endearing interactions between animals I have ever seen: The black Shepherd/Lab/Coyote mix was lying with his paw over what looked to be an incredibly mangy Pitbull mix who had electrical wires wrapped around her neck. He was licking her face and ears, trying to heal her mange. Her head was thrown back in total contentment and trust. I sat there for a few minutes wondering how I was going to rescue these lovebirds. The black dog was definitely one of the three feral landfill dogs, but perhaps the female was sweet and unafraid. Maybe I could get her easily. If I could, then it might be possible to lure the black dog using her as bait. The feral dog was totally smitten with the Pit mix, so I assumed she was in heat. The plan seemed plausible, but I needed to get her before she got pregnant and had her babies out there. I left a bowl of food and water so they would stay in the area, and went home to make a plan. The purebred Shepherd was nowhere to be seen.

"Eldad, I need your help. Can you meet me tomorrow at the landfill?"

Eldad Hagar, from Hope For Paws, is a baby-faced, lanky, ex-Israeli soldier, and one of my close rescue friends. Like me, he was really good at getting dogs that most people couldn't catch, but now he's even better at it than I am. The year before, while we were rescuing a scared puppy together, I had suggested Eldad start filming himself on his missions, as most people had never seen the things rescuers go through to capture a dog. He took my suggestion and eventually had a handful of videos on line. Now, four years and many videos later, he has an enormous fan base, and people fly him around the country to get dogs no one else can.

At nine o'clock the next morning, Eldad, his camera, and his friend Jaime Ray Newman showed up to help me. Jaime is an actress I had recently met who had done a film with my husband.

Luckily, the dogs were still there. Before we made a move, we named them: Jaime thought of "Millie" for the Pitbull girl, and because we were in the Shadow Hills/Sun Valley region and he was black, I named the feral one "Shadow," a name I had always thought generic, but now seemed fitting.

As we crept closer to them, the plan was to see if Millie would come to us. Eldad held a hamburger in his hand, and when the dogs smelled the meat and us, Shadow ran to the other side of the lot. But Millie approached. It was the first good look we had of her. She was a mess. Lisa had been correct: Millie had a skin condition called mange, which leads to hair loss and horrible secondary skin infections all over the body. It was obvious this poor dog was in deep physical distress. She had been severely neglected and then either dumped or got away.

Millie wanted the hamburger that Eldad held out, yet she growled at him out of fear. Obviously, this dog had never known human kindness. So we set a trap, using bits of meat to lure her inside. Five minutes later, she was trapped. Next we worked on a way to corner Shadow, using his girlfriend as bait. While still in the trap, we put her in the garbage area and tied the doors with rope, hoping that Shadow would enter and we would then pull the rope to trap him inside. But it didn't work. He was too scared and would not come back to our end of the lot.

As we loaded Millie into Eldad's SUV, I called out to Shadow, assuring the feral dog we would be back to get him. We left ample food and water, then off to the vet we went with Millie.

Nine times out of ten when we rescue dogs who are afraid of people, the dogs soon realize you want to help them and the tail wagging and kissing begins. Millie was no exception, even though she felt miserable from the infection all over her body. The vet immediately started her on medication, after agreeing she had a bad case of non-contagious demodectic mange.

The next morning at six I picked up Millie at the vet and met Eldad at the truck rental company before it opened. Shadow was there, waiting for us, and was *so* excited when he saw his girlfriend in my car. He followed as I pulled out of the lot onto the quiet street. I then stopped, leaned into the backseat, and opened the door, hoping he would jump inside with Millie. But that would have been a complete miracle, as Shadow was a feral dog and had never known a human, much less been inside a car. So I got Millie out, and we started walking toward Lisa's house (she had given us permission to use her backyard) at the end of the road. I was thrilled when the beautiful black canine followed us, and I remember thinking: *I'm about to rescue one of the feral dogs without a trap.* My body was shaking with excitement.

Once we got to Lisa's house, I tied Millie to a fence at the far end of the yard and then walked out, leaving the gate open. Eldad and I then crossed the street and hid behind a tree. A minute later, Shadow came running around the corner and into the yard, eager to see his girl. *Oh my god, it's really going to happen!* I quietly ran to shut the gate, only to start trembling once it was closed. The prospect of walking into the yard and seeing Shadow up close for the first time was incredibly exciting. Eldad was behind me as we carefully opened the gate and slipped inside.

Millie, thrilled to be back with her boyfriend, was wiggling her now clean, yet still mangy body, in the joyful way we had come to know since rescuing her the night before. Shadow, however, was terrified when he saw us walk in. He ran to the side of the yard and did his best to hide behind some fencing that was leaning against the wall. I walked over to Millie and untied her, and together we approached the frightened stray. Lisa, her dog Lola, and Billy had their heads through the window of the house, watching the whole encounter.

Luckily, Shadow's fear was turned inward and not outward on us. When Eldad reached his hand out to pet him, we found out very quickly that Shadow was not a biter. Unlike myself, Eldad does not have much fear of being bitten. In the past, he has put himself in some precarious situations, but this was not one of them. Within a half hour we were able to ease Shadow into a crate and begin the drive to the vet's office, where he was sedated, examined, bathed, neutered, chipped, and given his shots. Because Millie was in heat and in such poor health from the mange, she had to wait a few weeks before she could be spayed.

If you are interested in seeing Millie and Shadow's rescue video, you can go to my website, www.sylvakelegian.com. To see Eldad's other emotionally exciting videos, including the famous "Miley and Frankie," check out www. HopeForPaws.org.

Millie is the most joyful dog I have ever known, but if the DNA test her new family did on her is correct, she is not a Pitbull mix. The test claims she is a Shar Pei/Manchester Terrier/Chesapeake Bay Retriever mix. But God only knows the truth. Friends of mine, Deidre and her husband, Brad, adopted her. They also adopted one of Shadow's sisters, Beauty, from me two years before, and they have a Pitbull named Bo who I had rescued before he was dumped at the shelter.

After Shadow was released from the vet, I put him in a boarding facility where I could work with him. His neck was ripped up from going in and out of the barbed wire fence at the landfill, so we had to wait a month to put a collar on and train him. Many a day I would just sit in his kennel run, getting him to trust me. I'll never forget the look on Shadow's face when Eldad put a leash on him for the first time. Absolute fear and horror, yet he never tried to bite. It took me another month of daily visits and work on his socialization skills around the facility before he was ready to walk outside on leash . . . a day that was scary for both of us. I used two soft chokes and two leashes in case one of them slipped off.

Deidre brought Millie to visit Shadow a few times a week. Millie would lick her boyfriend's face, assuring him everything was okay, like he had licked her under the truck that day in an attempt to heal her mange. And slowly but surely, he came out of his shell. Through *her* trust in us, Millie showed Shadow that *he* could trust us as well. It was because of Millie that Shadow was rescued, and now she was teaching him that we were not to be feared.

As for the purebred German Shepherd that Lisa had seen with them: I went back every day that week until I found him and lured him into my car with some chicken. He was terrified, and in bad shape, with burns on his back. He probably had been an auto shop watchdog who had been dumped or escaped. He had no ID and was not neutered or microchipped. It was time for him to have a great life.

I had reached out to Maria at German Shepherd Rescue of Orange County when I first found out about the dog, and she was waiting to take him in. Maria is a great rescuer and does home checks, so I trusted her. Within two weeks, after he was medically treated, he was adopted by one of her volunteers and now lives with another Shepherd in a loving home.

I placed Billy, the dog from the balcony, who it turned out was an American Bulldog/Boxer, in his forever home with his new mom Gayla. She worked out of her house and lived near Runyon Canyon, so Billy would get tons of exercise, and be her constant companion.

My hope was to send Shadow to the Best Friends Animal Sanctuary located in Kanab, Utah. I had visited the Sanctuary some years before, when Jude and I had taken a trip to Utah to see a friend of his whose wife worked there. We were given a tour of the amazing property and met two of the founders, Cyrus and Francis. After I rescued from death row a Shepherd/Cattle Dog, who I soon discovered was an escape artist with the worst separation anxiety I had ever seen, I contacted Cyrus for help. This dog, Pearl, not only broke out of a crate, but also managed to crawl out of my foster's high, closed bathroom window. So off to Best Friends she went. Sammy and I drove her, and we stayed overnight in one of their lovely bungalows. The next day we made the seven-hour return trip.

People come from all over the world to visit Best Friends Animal Sanctuary. Pearl was adopted by Susan and Ray Hearon, from Colorado, and re-named Chaco. They had experienced separation anxiety with one of their other dogs and were able to deal with Chaco's behavior by putting her in their garage (with another dog) that had steel siding when they were gone, which was not often. I was told she did climb on Ray's Harley once and got out the window. But a year after being with them, Chaco knew she was *home* and her anxiety went away. They kept in touch with me and let me know of her passing some five years later.

When I first rescued Shadow, I reached out to Francis at Best Friends who said that if after my working with the feral dog he was well behaved enough around other dogs (which he was) and people, Best Friends might be able to take him in if they had room. Shadow was not adoptable, except to someone like me who could continue training him, so Best Friends would have been the perfect place for him to live and be socialized. After three months of my going almost every day to work with him, Shadow was ready to get out of boarding and experience his new life outside of a metal kennel run. But the timing was not good. The Sanctuary was full up and could not take him. People are clamoring to send animals from all over the country to Best Friends, and they only have room for so many, so I understood.

I knew that, given a chance, Shadow would run away. Whether escaping out of a loose collar or an open door, he would be gone. I couldn't take that chance. There was nobody else I trusted to keep him safe, except myself. So he became our dog.

After the Frankie incident, Jude was reluctant to have me bring Shadow home, but I assured him that *this* dog had no bite in him. At that point we had Beau Bo, Mazie, and Nate, a Cocker Spaniel/Dachshund mix who had been dumped at a Ford dealership car lot. Nate had waited a year for his owner to return, but that never happened. Dealership workers and neighbors had fed him, but no one could get near him, not even animal control. It broke my heart to see the little black dog sit on the corner and watch people go in and out of the vet's office across the street with their dogs. He just wanted his own person. He was a smart boy and wouldn't go in a trap. I spent two weeks going two times a day to befriend him, until I got him eating out of my hand. But when I got the loop leash out, he would back up. I eventually had to drug him with some doggy sleeping pills, which made his true feelings come out—he wanted my help. He allowed me to reach out to pet him as I threw the loop over his head.

The day after Christmas of that year, our dearest Beau Bo, my Little Handsome, passed away at nineteen years of age. The dog who we originally thought had only one more year in him had lived another *ten* happy years with us. He was our special boy, and we loved him so. Our proud Terrier had not been well for a long time, but had not wanted to leave us. He hung in there until his body gave out and that last night I rocked him in my arms for an hour before we put him to sleep. One more fur child gone from our lives.

It's been almost four years since Shadow came to live with us. With me, he is now a normal dog. And though he can still be a bit wary of Jude, they do love each other. This, at one time, feral, outdoor dog, has never gone to the bathroom in our house (which is more than I can say for Nate), loves giving kisses to us and our guests, has a joyful personality (like Millie), is highly intelligent, runs like a pony, and is a great player with other dogs. Shadow also likes to play with me. His favorite thing is to have me bang on his butt like I'm playing the bongos, while he puts the front half of his body on the ground and sticks his bottom in the air. "Shady" is also the best leash walker in town. Stays right by my side. But planes heard in the distance make him jittery and children freak him out. So, at the end of our walks, he's very happy when we get home and I shut the door behind us, blocking out the scary world. At night he stays in our bed beside me until Jude, who goes to sleep later than I, comes into the room. Then my landfill dog jumps down and spends the rest of the evening in his own, large, soft bed, next to Mazie and Nate.

Shadow trusts his mama and lets me bathe him, but he hates to have his nails cut, so I let our vet, Dr. Sharp, do it. My beautiful black boy used to freeze and not protest, but lately he is standing up for himself. The crying now starts the minute we pull into the parking lot, and on the vet table he fights with all his might to get out of the noose around his neck as I hold my "bucking Stallion" and try to calm him.

Sometimes, at home, "Shady" looks at me out of the corner of his eye and smiles, and I smile back and say, "I'm very proud of you, my 'Shaboo.' You're my brave boy, and I love you."

I was never able to rescue Shadow's last two brothers. A year later they had not been seen by any of the landfill workers, so Eldad and I put a camera near the food bowl to see if they were still there. But all we captured on the video were coyotes enjoying the kibble.

Unfortunately, it did not work out for Shadow and his girlfriend, Millicent (as I call her), to live together. However, they have play dates at our house, where they greet each other like the lovers they were and the best friends they are now.

Love, I say to myself as I sit and watch them run and play, chew and kiss. *That's Love.*

CHAPTER FIFTEEN

Saving Gracie

When you rescue and find homes for over five hundred dogs like I have, the odds are something will go wrong with at least one of them. Sadly, that was the case with Elsa.

It was the week before Christmas and I was sitting in my car on Mandeville Canyon, an upscale area in Los Angeles, surrounded by hills and canyons. I had just driven around for the fifteenth time looking for Elsa, who had been adopted the year before and was now missing. The man she was bonded to had gone into the hospital, and his wife had left the front door ajar at the same time the security gate was open and she had run away. A few other rescue people who loved her were looking as well.

Elsa had disappeared six days before and during that time, I had not had much sleep. My stomach ached with anxiety. It was strange; just a few days before she ran away, I had told myself how lucky I was to never have had a dog that I rescued go missing. Maybe if I had not had that thought, it would never have happened. Or maybe I knew what was coming, so the thought came first?

Either way, it was heartbreaking! Truly devastating for all of us, but especially for James Symington and me. James was an ex-Canadian cop who, along with his dog Trakr, had been at Ground Zero rescuing people after September 11th. He and his lovely wife, Angeline, had not only helped me rescue Elsa, but had also fostered her before she got adopted.

Elsa had been living on the streets for years without anyone being able to touch her. I spent months trying to get this 40-pound, dainty, white Shepherd, mixed with a hint of something wild, perhaps coyote. She would not go into a trap, so we ultimately had to drug her. And six of us, including fellow rescuer Suzanne Happ, had run Elsa down, guiding her along, until she ran into a loop leash that Angeline held out. It was a miracle. Two centimeters one side or the other and she would have escaped.

Almost a year later, Elsa was out there again, all alone. She had never really come around to being the pet the retired couple had hoped she would become, though she loved her daily walks with the man and slept in their room. But even after warning them many times never to give her the opportunity to run off, our worst fear had come true. She had gotten out and had last been seen four days before in the middle of a quiet road. This was coyote territory, and she was not big or strong enough to protect herself against a pack.

I prayed again for the hundredth time that day: *Please, God, let us find her. Let someone see one of our three hundred flyers out there and call with a sighting.* Angry, I pounded the dashboard with my fists. *Why did this have to happen to Elsa and why do animals have to suffer so? I can't take it anymore, God, I really can't take it anymore. I wish I didn't care so much. Why do I have to care so much?*

I had not just lost Elsa; I was beginning to lose my faith. *Why did this have to happen to this very sweet, shy dog after all she had been through? I need a miracle, God,* I prayed. *Please perform a miracle for Elsa!*

And then my phone rang. "Hello!" I screamed into it when I didn't recognize the number.

"Hi, I saw your flyer, and I think I have your dog."

"What! Where?"

"I live in Encino, and a white dog has been living on the street here for a few days and now she's in my backyard."

My heart was beating out of my chest. We had put up flyers in Encino. If she had gotten over the canyon she could be there. "But she's terrified of people," I said. "How did you get her?"

"I lured her in with some food."

Could be, I thought as I started my car and headed back to Sunset to catch the freeway. We had been getting calls all week from people thinking they had found her, but it was never Elsa. This sounded like it could actually be her. My hand was shaking as I rang the doorbell. *Please, God, let it be her.*

As the saying goes, when one door closes, another door opens. I walked out to the backyard and there were two dogs: a brown Lab and a white Terrier, who was the same size as Elsa—but was not Elsa. She was just as endearing, with adoring brown eyes, and she looked like a movie dog. But she was *not* Elsa.

"She's been roaming the neighborhood for a while," the guy said as he pointed to her ribs and dirty body. "She needs help."

I then realized this man knew she was *not* Elsa, but he hadn't known what to do so he lured me in too. "Why don't you keep her?" I sighed. "She seems to get along with your dog."

"Because she bit my landlord on the leg when he came over today, and he won't let me."

Oh, great, not just another dog to rescue, but a biting one! I couldn't take on another Frankie. The white Terrier looked at me, came over, and rubbed her head against my leg. She was beautiful and adorable. I think she knew if she bit me, she wouldn't stand a chance. I knelt down to pet her pretty, soft head, and she kissed my cheek. "How bad was the bite?" I asked.

"Not bad. Just a little nip."

"Okay. I'll take her." She was now a rescued dog, thanks to Elsa. The phone calls eventually stopped and the flyers faded months before we gave up on her, but the question of Elsa's fate was always in the back of my mind. We took Gracie, the white Terrier's new name, to dog adoptions on the weekend, where she nipped a potential adopter in the face. It wasn't a bad nip, but bad enough to make him rethink adopting her.

James and Angeline, who were by now fostering Gracie, decided not to bring her to adoptions anymore, and I agreed. None of us needed a lawsuit. We'd have to find her home through the internet and flyers.

Those people came to us pretty quickly from Petfinder, a website for animals who are up for adoption. Amanda and Thom were a couple in their thirties who lived in a hip loft downtown. Their Terrier had recently passed away. I described Gracie's behavior, as I always divulge everything about a dog before the meet and greet, but I assured Amanda that Gracie would not bite them if I brought her to their apartment. "She only gets defensive on leash, like at dog adoptions or when someone comes on her territory who she doesn't trust, like the landlord," I said.

It was such familiar behavior to me by now, but at least she didn't attack people, like Frankie did. Amanda and Thom were not afraid. I was thrilled.

I drove with Gracie downtown to their loft the next day. It was love at first sight for all of them. I knew instantly that the Terrier had found her family. After doing this for years, I've come to know the signs pretty quickly.

However, a few weeks later I got a call. The little miss was pushing them to consider giving her back to us. Gracie had been kicked out of doggy day care after she tried to bite the owner, and she had lunged at their parking lot attendant, as well as people on the street. "I'm not sure we can keep her," Amanda said to me. "She might be a liability."

I totally understood and began second-guessing myself, thinking that I had made a mistake placing Gracie in that type of environment. In the loft, she had to go out into the world and be walked four times a day, and would most likely have been better off in a house where she could go in and out whenever she wanted through a doggy door. I thought by socializing her the issue could be worked on, but I was wrong.

"Give us a few days," Amanda said. "We'll get back to you when we make a decision."

The call came a few days later, but it was not the call I thought it was going to be. I was at dinner with my dear friend Laura Tressel, and her daughters, Kate and Anna, when I checked in to see if I had messages regarding an audition the next day. "Hi, Sylva," a panicked voice said. "Gracie is gone. The dog walker had the leash attached to her collar, she slipped out, and she's gone. We've been looking since noon and we can't find her. I hate to call and ruin your night, but we are at a loss and out of our minds with worry!"

I sat there listening to the message. It was like *déjà vu*. *Was Gracie meant to follow Elsa's path?* I wondered. *How could this be happening again?* I had never had one of my dogs go missing before Elsa and now, incredibly, Gracie too? I realized there was nothing I could do because it was already dark. I called her back. "I can't come tonight. Keep looking for her and put up flyers everywhere saying 'reward.' I'll be there first thing in the morning." I felt terrible for them, horrible for Gracie, and frustrated that I was in this position again. Lost in the vast downtown Los Angeles area, Gracie could have gone anywhere, been cornered by anyone and taken, or hit by a car. But I didn't feel that I would find her if I tried that night. I felt that she was most likely hiding out somewhere until morning, unless someone had her.

I lay in bed, tossing and turning. I had been ignoring God lately and relying on myself too much. *Please have Gracie home by tomorrow*, I prayed. *We need a miracle.*

Because the dog walker had attached the leash to her collar instead of her nylon choke chain, the collar, which had Gracie's identification tags on it, had slipped over her head. She had run away without any ID and now had little chance of getting home, unless someone found her and either saw the flyer, or was able to scan her for a microchip, which was registered to Amanda and me—but that was a long shot. The dog walker had been fired on the spot from the dog walking company for not following Amanda and Thom's rule of never walking their Terrier on a collar.

Please, God, we need a miracle!

At seven o'clock the next morning, I drove downtown to look for Gracie. I spent a few hours driving around the area—then walking and talking to people, showing them Gracie's picture (with her new haircut/shave) on a flyer that Thom had e-mailed to me the night before. No one had seen her.

Amanda and Thom had to go to work, but Amanda had called a dog psychic, who told her that Gracie was on the outskirts of town in a residential, hilly area near a freeway. That was miles away from where I was looking, so Amanda told me which way to go. I headed to the end of downtown, toward a hilly area which happened to be Chinatown, but had no luck. After a few more hours I felt hopeless, so I went to the gym and then stopped for lunch at Chipotle, my favorite food addiction at the time. It was the middle of the day, and Amanda had by now left work and was putting up flyers with the added "Reward" in the Chinatown area.

While I was eating my burrito, I had an enormous feeling that I needed to go back. I felt that if I didn't leave right then and there, we would never find Gracie. It was a very strong feeling. *Thank you, God, for leading us to her,* I prayed as I drove back downtown, confident she would be found. I had learned that when you pray as if it's already happened, your success rate is better.

Amanda and I met up below Chinatown and posted more flyers. She was in her work clothes and heels, and had not slept either. I felt sorry for her, as I knew she adored this dog and was heartbroken. I had to pee, which turned out to be quite important, yielding the following drama. I headed into an office building to use the bathroom. When I came out, we went back to Chinatown and pulled up in front of a restaurant in the hilly area near the freeway. I got out of the car, held up a flyer, and asked the people sitting outside if they had seen Gracie.

No one had, but as I said, "Have you seen this dog?" a construction worker came out of the restaurant at that exact moment and asked, "Is it a white dog?"

"YES!" Amanda and I both screamed!

"My foreman saw a white dog limping near our site yesterday. She was bleeding."

I didn't bother to ask why he hadn't helped her. No reason would have been good enough. "WHERE?" we screamed again.

"Follow me," he said.

Off we went toward the hilly streets, up and down and at least a mile away, where we would have never looked.

We pulled up and showed the foreman our flyer. "That's the dog," he said.

Oh, why didn't you help her? I wanted to yell at him! But instead I asked, "Where was she?" He pointed across the street. We ran over to look, and there was a trail of blood leading from the street to the sidewalk. I had never been so happy to see blood! *Oh, Gracie! What happened and where are you? Thank you, God, for leading us to her.* My body was shaking, and my heart was pounding in my chest. I was both hopeful and terrified at the same time.

Amanda jumped in her car and drove slowly behind me as I ran down the sidewalk following the blood trail, which led to an abandoned building that was next to the freeway. In my gut, I knew Gracie was there.

Behind the building, I only saw garbage butting up against the freeway fence. I stood there for a moment wondering where she could have gone. Perhaps someone had cornered Gracie back here and taken her? Just as I was about to walk away, something caught my eye on the right side as I turned. A bush, which must have started as a weed and had grown through a cement crack, surrounded something gray. When I walked closer I saw her. Curled up in a ball and probably waiting to die, was a terrified, dirty, gray Gracie! "AMANDA! SHE'S HERE!" I shouted so loud I probably scared the whole neighborhood.

As Amanda came running toward us, I made a loop with my leash and slipped it over Gracie's neck, gently pulling her out from under the bush. She could barely walk, but she was alive and happy to be found. *What a fucking miracle*, I whispered to myself. Gracie wrapped her paws around Amanda and gave her mother grateful, loving kisses. And then off to the vet we went.

The owner of the dog-walking business met us there looking very sheepish, but he picked up the cost of the veterinary care. The pads on each of Gracie's feet had been ripped off, probably from stepping on glass, but she had no broken bones and nothing internally wrong. Her paws would heal after a month of bandage changes and being pampered. "By the way," Amanda said as we were leaving the vet. "We won't be giving her back. We will make it work. No matter what happens, we'll make it work. She's our Gracie, and we're keeping her."

I laughed to myself. What a journey the Terrier had to take to keep her home. *Thank you, God. Thank you so much for this miracle. And thank you dog psychic Joan Ranquet for leading us to the right area.* Had we pulled up one minute earlier or later, the construction worker wouldn't have heard me say, "Have you seen this dog?" And we would never have found her.

It broke my heart that we didn't find Elsa. I think the coyotes got her. She was a wild girl and as painful as it is for me to accept, it must have been her destiny to end her journey in that canyon.

Did Elsa have to disappear so that Gracie was rescued? I'll never know. Though I have learned I can't save the world, God did let me know He was listening that day, and another white dog *was* rescued . . . twice . . . and my faith restored, once again.

My initials on the landfill tarp

Millie with mange

Shadow (with hurt neck) & me

Tee & Dad, photographer Frank Bruynbroek

Shadow at home

Millie & Family

Gayla & Billy

Nate

Pearl (lying down) and Family

Sylva, Suzanne, Angeline, James and Elsa

Have you seen me?

My name is Gracie & I'm missing

Gracie flyer

CHAPTER SIXTEEN

Fur Children

Saving a dog won't change the world, but it will change the world for that one dog. Every animal I have ever rescued is just as important as the next, but some stories are more compelling than others:

Tyson, the gentle, loving, Blue Nose Pit, was kept in a 4×4 garbage area for the first year of his life. For months, we tried to educate the man who had bought Ty as a puppy, but that did no good. Finally, the Foundation paid a great deal of money to make the inhumane owner give up his dog. Tyson is now with the Jennings-Benzo family and walked every day, with his two sisters, a Chihuahua and a Bulldog, who like to share his bed. He is cherished and appreciated.

Lady is a little, loving Terrier mix who I rescued off the streets of Miami in front of her house while I was on vacation. She was covered from head to toe with ticks and allowed to roam the streets. I told her owners I would turn them in to animal control if they didn't let me take her and made them promise to never get another dog. I warned them that my friends, who lived down the street, would be watching. Some people might think, How dare you say that? But sometimes it's the only way to scare someone who neglects animals and will do it again and again if they think they can get away with it. After she was looked at by a vet, Lady drove with me from Miami to Anna Maria. Then we flew back to LA, where I took her on the *Good Day L.A.* pet segment. She was later adopted into her forever home with the Lisi family.

Holly is a feisty little black-and-white Terrier mix who I spotted on the streets of Hollywood one night, on my way to do a play, and spent two weeks trying to catch. The morning some other rescue gals and I caught her, I had awakened thanking God, knowing that "today was the day." I used my "thank you first and then see the miracle happen" way of praying. Sure enough, it worked. As I was wandering the area, I happened to ask a guy coming out of a building if he had seen her. Lo and behold, he led me behind the building where she was hiding. We cornered her, and she is now living with another dog and great parents, Craig and Jennifer, in Burbank.

Then there was Jesse, the soulful, beaten-down Australian Shepherd mix who was hit by a car, left in front of his house for years, and never taken to a vet. He could barely walk when another woman and I removed him from that neglectful home. I papered the equestrian neighborhood with two hundred flyers, knowing only a selfless animal person would want him. Two days later, he was adopted by Jenna and Chris Nelson, who got him physical therapy and swam with him in their pool to heal his legs, until he died a few months later. But he finally knew what it was like to be cared for.

And there is Benny, the smart, loving, deaf, limping, separation-anxiety Pitbull/Boxer/Great Dane mix who fellow rescuer Pamela Curran saved from the streets and that Linzi and I took on. Six months later, after working with his foster/trainer, he became a calm dog and now has a wonderful forever home with the Mathews family.

Nicki was the most matted Poodle I had ever seen in my life. I rescued her, her puppies, and three other dogs from the streets of San Fernando with rescuer-in-training Kate Gleason. Nicki had a family who let her wander and never bathed or groomed her. She is now a spoiled rotten daddy's girl, living with Jude's bandmates, Craig and Candy, and their Chihuahuas.

The beautiful Devore girls, Tessa and Polly (dogs I would have kept if I could), who came from that high kill shelter, are a testament to the saying, "What's meant to be will be." I had made a decision *not* to rescue any more dogs for a while when, in January, I was sent a plea for Tessa. Her beautiful, intelligent, kind face drew me to her. She was being called a small Leonberger or Aussie mix, but once I got her I figured her to be a Belgian Malinois/Golden Retriever mix. She had the Malinois coloring and intelligence, combined with Retriever hair and loving personality.

I placed Tessa in a foster home with Ryan McDermott and Sabi, a young couple who had recently signed record deals and were heavily immersed in their artistic endeavors. Though they loved Tessa dearly, they were too busy to adopt a dog but offered to keep her until I found the right home.

Through Petfinder, I got thirty calls in the first few weeks from people wanting the beautiful girl. Unfortunately, only one of them felt like the right home. However, they had six-foot walls surrounding their house, and the second day Tessa was there, she tried to scale the back yard wall to go after a squirrel. Luckily the people were there. If she had gotten over, she could have been hit by a car on the busy street. They returned her.

Though Tessa loved to play with other dogs at the dog park, she preferred to be the only dog in a home, as she wanted the attention all to herself. Her options were dwindling . . . she had to have unusually tall fences or live in an apartment and in either case would be best as an only dog. The calls kept coming, but all the good homes fell through for one reason or another. In March I got an email from a woman named Krista who sounded like a great candidate, but she wasn't moving into her new home until May. I also got a call from a young gal named Catherine who was moving into *her* new home within the month. At the same time, I received a call from a retired couple in Santa Barbara who sounded great. So now I had some options. I decided to try the Santa Barbara couple, but within two days she was returned again. Tessa had no problem being alone at Ryan and Sabi's, but for some reason she got a bit destructive in Santa Barbara. Once again . . . not meant to be. Back to the fosters she went, until Catherine was ready for her. But after Tessa was with Catherine for a few weeks, the young gal realized she was not up for having a big dog after all. However, she *was* willing to foster until Krista could take her.

I have come to realize that the right home is always out there, but sometimes the people are not ready when we are, and the animals and I have to be patient.

Tessa is now Krista's constant companion (she can take her to work) and the center of attention, which is what the very special Malinois/Golden needed. And she gets to play with other dogs at the park.

A few months after pulling Tessa, I had seen another plea for a dog that reminded me of Sammy. A stunning Shepherd/Collie mix at Devore. I called the shelter and was told she was in such high demand that on the morning she became available there would be a bidding war for her. I bowed out and prayed that whatever was best for the gorgeous dog would happen. At noon, on the day she was available, I called to see who had adopted her and was informed she was still there. *Nobody* had shown up that morning to get her! I laughed . . . I guess *I* was the "best" person to pull her. I knew I would put her in the right home.

My dear friend Ellen Gerstein fostered her and put the word out to her friends. Through Robin Lippin, she was brought to the attention of Jo and Bill LaMond, who had two large male dogs. The boys had had some tussles in the past and had worked through them, so Jo wasn't sure bringing in a female, that they could fight over, would be the smartest thing to do. I liked Jo immediately and got a good feeling about the home. We decided to try it . . . and it worked. Instead of the dogs *fighting* over her, Miss "Polly" Crackers has brought *harmony* to the house. The boys adore her and share the beauty girl without any problems.

Living in LA as I do, I have adopted to celebrities: Rainn Wilson and his lovely wife, Holiday, have had four Pitbulls through me. Amy Adams and her boyfriend Darren have Sadie, a Miniature Pinscher/Chihuahua mix who I rescued from death row along with her mother and siblings. Allison Janney adopted Addie, an adorable Cattle Dog puppy who I got from a hoarding situation. The guy was busted for having over two hundred animals living in filthy, neglectful conditions. And Danny, a handsome, yellow Hound dog who came from death row and was going to be put down because of kennel cough and a hurt leg. He went from the high-kill, Kern County animal shelter to living with Laurence Mark, one of the biggest producers in Hollywood.

And then there was Charlie. My friends Peter and Marylou called to tell me that their potential landlord wanted to meet their crazy, jumping, barking dog that I had helped them adopt years before. "They will never allow us to rent the house with Charlie. They're not dog lovers, he's too hyperactive, and we don't know what to do," they said.

I was over there the next day with a dose of doggy Xanax, which gave Charlie a calm, sleepy demeanor during the home interview. Half of this town is pretending to be something they're not, so I didn't think it would hurt if Charlie did it for a few hours.

"What a good, easy dog," the landlord said.

They got the house, and Charlie was back to his old self the next day.

I rescued a dog from the street last year. I pulled over when I saw him on the side of the road and got out my bag of treats and loop leash that I keep in my car at all times. He was a purebred dog in a shitty neighborhood. He was filthy, and his nails were so long and curled under he could barely walk. He was not neutered and did not have an ID tag or a microchip.

Some people would try to find the dog's owner. They might say: "Maybe the owner doesn't know about neutering or cutting nails. Maybe there is a person out there who is missing that dog." But I don't think like that anymore. I have seen too much. I've witnessed abuse and neglect beyond comprehension, so if I can give an animal the chance for a better life, I make that happen. That's why, after neutering and vetting him, I found that dog another home. He now has a wading pool, a large yard, and a king-sized bed to sleep in with his new parents and their two other dogs. Besides playing with his siblings all day, he gets a walk, plus all the love and attention he deserves.

The archaic law says that dogs are property; that they should be returned to their owner. To me they are not property. They are souls with feelings who don't deserve to suffer to make a person happy. If the animal movement keeps heading in the direction it's going, I believe this law, and many other antiquated laws regarding animals, will be changed one day. Therefore, I have faith that by the time I leave this world, dogs and cats will be on the books as "family members," not property.

I truly wish that animals could talk and tell us about their journeys and how they were treated and discarded and what makes them the way they are today. Every one of them has a story. Just as we do.

Sometimes I look very closely at a dog. I examine their fur. I peer into their eyes. I touch their paws, their ears, and I wonder how we can waste God's creation. It's truly staggering when you stop to think about it. These creatures are non-judgmental, sentient, loving beings. Like all of us, they deserve to live up to their potential, to experience joy, and love, and freedom. Yet we are killing them by the millions because people keep breeding them. We are killing—love. Man's best friend.

It's been twelve years since I started rescuing. I have spent so much time with canines that I can now read their body language and their thoughts almost as well as they can read mine. And I do believe they read our thoughts. Dogs are more insightful and intuitive than humans give them credit for.

Years ago I realized I would do anything to help an animal. I value them all the same, whether they have homes or not, because they are like children and don't always get the best parent. When I see a dog left in a car or tied outside a store, I usually wait for the person or write a note explaining that their dog could be stolen, sold for research, used as Pitbull-fighting bait, or taken because someone wants a dog. Or just because somebody wants to screw up someone else's day. Dogs are stolen out of backyards, cars, and in front of stores on a daily basis. And when I see people walking their companions off leash on the street, I used to scream: "What the hell are you thinking?" Now, I pull over and hand them a piece of paper I keep in my car. It lists the bad things that can happen when your dog is off leash, such as them running into the street to be killed and a car swerving to miss the dog and killing a mother and child on the sidewalk instead, or your dog running up to another canine and being attacked. Handing them the paper saves me from getting into a shouting match and raising my blood pressure.

My trunk is full of dog paraphernalia, though very neatly organized in bags: leash bag, collar bag, halter/nylon choke bag. I also keep a loop leash and treats in my glove compartment in case I see a four-legged friend running loose.

I've been asked, "Why help animals and not people?" My answer is that I do help people: "Sylva, this dog has changed my life and I can't thank you enough," was the message I got from a retired man who adopted a senior dog I pulled from death row; and "I don't know what I would do without this fur child in my life," a single woman said to me a year after I placed a Chihuahua mix with her; and "We want to thank you for saving Max from the streets. The dogs are so in love, we can't believe it took us this long to get our dog a friend," the newlyweds said as they hugged me. And "I can't imagine them being split up. Thank you for keeping them together until we came along," from the couple that adopted a bonded pair that I had rescued and waited six months to find them a home together.

And I am happy for them. Not just for the dogs, but for the adopters as well.

Tyson & his brother

Lady

Holly & Family

Benny & Family

Nicki the day I rescued her

Nicki & Family

Krista and Tessa

Polly

Rainn, Holiday, Oona (the first pit they got through me)
and their beloved Harper Lee

Amy, Sadie & Darren

Allison & Addie

Larry & Danny

Peter, Marylou, Sophia, Charlie & Gracie

Linzi, Victoria and me with rescued dogs

EPILOGUE

These days, instead of rescuing so much, I am putting my energy into projects that I hope will raise awareness, like this book and the one-hour drama about the rescue world that I co-wrote for television. And I'm still a working actress.

Being a dog rescuer is a calling and a curse and I sometimes wish I had not been called. But it's given me a greater faith at times, and made me aware of all the wonderful people out there. And that, in itself, gives me hope.

Why do rescuers do it? Why do we put ourselves through it? *My* only answer is that once you're in it, it's very hard to get out. Very difficult to walk away. Very tough to turn your back on living beings who need your help. Like being sucked into quicksand, you feel the pull. But some of us have to get out. Rescue burnout is real, and it comes upon most of us who are in it long enough. It certainly did me.

As far as my faith goes, it's not God I don't trust, it's humanity, who have been given free rein. But I am trying to accept the things I cannot change, and I remind myself daily of Gandhi's quote: "There is nothing that wastes the body like worry, and one who has any faith in God should be ashamed to worry about anything whatsoever."

Some say the purpose of life is to attain great happiness—impossible, unless one can accept the world as it is. Others say the purpose is the expansion of happiness and the ability to love and have compassion. But when you love and have compassion, it's hard to accept the world as it is.

Instead of focusing on all those suffering, I now try to live in the moment, keep my focus on the very fortunate life I have, and look for the miracles—as difficult as that sometimes is.

When I turned my life over to the Lord years earlier, in the little brown church on Coldwater Canyon in Los Angeles, I prayed that He use me in some way. As I sat in the third pew on the right, looking up at the painting of Christ that was hanging above the altar, I assumed that things would be made easier for me—that I would be more fulfilled from then on. I never thought that I would be exposed to the dark side. Never believed that my journey would be more complicated, and that I would be used to help dogs, and in doing so, I would also help people.

In hindsight, I have to smile at the way my prayer was answered. To me, dogs are the closest beings to God—spirits who love unconditionally and have taught me to love them unconditionally.

Truly, DOG *IS* GOD, spelled backwards.

So when I'm questioned about why I rescue, I look at all the lives I have saved or made better and think, what else would I have done? Who would I be? I'd be an actress, a writer, and a wife who has a lovely home, wonderful friends, and a great social life. Maybe I would travel more, though as much as I love traveling, I have to stay away from cities and countries that don't honor their animals.

But I already am all the things I would be. The day I saw my Princess stumble down those stairs with her big ears and long tail, I never dreamed my life would take this turn. But it did and here I am.

I am an actress. I am a writer. I am a wife. And I am a dog rescuer.

My dearest Sammy—because of you, I am a dog rescuer.

After Thoughts

I had been rescuing for a few years when it dawned on me I could save a dog every day for the rest of my life and never make a dent in the overpopulation problem. The laws in our country are not written to help stop the breeding of animals. They are still legally considered "property," allowed to live in cages, or on chains, or in the freezing cold. We really are no better than a third-world country or the different cultures that treat animals like inanimate objects, not believing they have souls.

The majority of animals on this planet are suffering, and most dogs are living lonely lives in backyards without any companionship whatsoever. Canines are pack animals and more social than humans. Making a dog live alone in a yard is one of the cruelest things you can do to them.

The overcrowding in our city shelters is astounding, and I don't know how most of the workers bear it, as a lot of them are animal lovers. Shelter volunteers work tirelessly, taking pictures of dogs and cats and circulating them on the internet so the animals don't have to be put down. But sometimes it's better for the animals in the shelters than the ones being mistreated in homes, or on the streets, starving, or being hit by cars.

I used to be horrified by the fact that an animal would die in the shelter. It still breaks my heart, but I would rather see a dog put down than neglected or abused. I no longer think death is such a bad thing, when you compare it to the heartbreak and misery some souls have to go through. To me, quality of life is more important than quantity, especially when it comes to animals. I also used to gasp at the thought of aborting a dog or cat. I now believe in it. There are too many wonderful creatures with horrible lives. If stopping more from being born gives those that are already here a chance, I now say, yes.

Just one unaltered female dog and her offspring can produce 67,000 puppies in only six years. In seven years, one female cat and her offspring can produce 420,000 kittens! Only one in twelve of those cats born finds a home. Los Angeles is trying to have a "No Kill" policy in local shelters but without first enforcing spay/neuter, that is impossible. The spay/neuter law is being fought all over the country because breeders want the right to breed, and puppy mills want the right to keep dogs in cages, year after year, litter after litter, so they can churn out cute puppies to sell. All the while, the breeding parents suffer terribly, never knowing kindness or even what it feels like to live outside of a wire cage. And we allow it. We allow dogs to be kept in cages, where they can barely stand up and turn around. We allow it in this country and it's horribly, horribly wrong. Because of some wonderful animal activists (led by Best Friends Animal Sanctuary) who have petitioned at pet stores and gone in front of city council meetings in California, certain cities have passed a law that puppies from puppy mills cannot be sold in pet stores. In Burbank, I joined my fellow activists and spoke at our council meeting and eventually, because of a handful of animal lovers who did not back down, Burbank no longer allows them to be sold. We followed other cities in our area like Hollywood and Glendale. If every city in the United States passed this law, puppy mills would be out of business, and the misery would end for thousands and thousands of dogs. Joey Herrick, one of the original owners of Natural Balance dog food, has started The Lucy Pet Foundation. The Foundation has a low-cost spay/neuter van in Los Angeles and hopes to be nationwide in the near future. And Sam Simon, one of the creators of *The Simpsons,* has free spay/neuter vans (The Sam Simon Foundation) that go all over Los Angeles for low-income animal owners. Fixing your dogs can also help prevent them from getting cancer. Dogs spayed before experiencing their first heat cycle have a 0.5% chance of developing mammary cancer. This increases to 8% if they experience one heat cycle and 26% if they go through two heat cycles. Males also have a high chance of getting cancer (testicular) if they are not neutered. Every time I read about a Pitbull attack in the news, I am devastated for the victims and so very sad for the dogs, who are usually un-neutered, which causes their hormones to rage and can increase aggressiveness. Very often, these dogs are kept on chains or pent up in back yards. If people would stop treating their Pitbulls like property, get them fixed, socialize them, and give them the exercise they need, my feeling is that these attacks would lessen greatly.

There is a wonderful camaraderie between my rescue friends and me, a shared calling, and a true understanding of what we all go through. Not only are there rescue groups for all kinds of mixed breeds but for every purebred dog as well, because so many people buy purebred dogs only to dump them later. Hundreds of rescue groups and individuals are spending their time, energy, and money to help our neglected and abused four-legged friends. Rescuers all over the country give up their weekends to drive dogs and cats to adoption events in hopes of finding each animal a good home. I have done adoptions almost every Sunday for twelve years. The last six years I have shown in Pacific Palisades with my dear friend, casting director Victoria Burrows from Starpaws Rescue. Besides the time we put in for adoption events, we also spend countless hours listing dogs on the internet, making flyers that we post all over town, and driving to do home checks. I have been in many, many homes, and it's fascinating how people's living spaces are so different. Though I love my clean house, I always let potential adopters know the only thing I am looking for in theirs is to make sure the environment is safe for the animal. Unfortunately, not all rescue people do it for the right reasons, and some become hoarders or will give a dog to anyone who coughs up the adoption fee. To me, a great rescuer is someone who fixes, chips, and vets the animal, keeps an ID tag on the dog or cat at all times, and then does a home check to make sure the animal is in the right environment as an indoor pet. Rescue should be about the animals' needs, not our own. What is best for the animal is what we in rescue need to remember. Always do what is best for the animal. As Abraham Lincoln said, "I am in favor of animal rights as well as human rights. That is the way of a whole human being."

The dogs, cats, monkeys and mice being tormented in experiments conducted in the name of helping humans is appalling. Most of them are abused horribly for the sake of justifying the money put into research; research that, in the big picture, most often doesn't help anyone. As Gandhi also said, "The greatness of a nation and its moral progress can be judged by the way its animals are treated." In 2012, $53 billion was spent on food, vetting, grooming, boarding at pet hotels, pet sitting, and daycare. So there are a lot of dog lovers out there. A movement has started. Animal lovers are making a difference. It's just not enough—not yet.

Good Dog Owner Rules

1. Always have identification on your animal, even inside your house. You never know when they might escape.
2. Get your animal fixed and microchipped, and register the chip to yourself and someone you trust.
3. Walk a dog on a choke or harness. Never attach a leash to a collar, which can easily slip off, leaving the dog without any visible identification.
4. Never walk a dog off leash on the streets.
5. Never leave a dog unattended in a car or tied outside a store. Cars get too hot. Too many pets have been stolen.
6. Exercise your dog daily.
7. Dogs are social animals and should live inside your house, not outside.
8. Never drive with a window open wide enough that your dog might jump out to chase a cat or squirrel.
9. When trimming a dog's nails, use a muzzle, even with dogs that have never shown any aggression.
10. When trying to catch a dog, never chase them. Generally, it's best to kneel and put chicken or treats down and lure them.
11. Dogs that have not been spayed or neutered should not be taken to dog parks. Other dogs too often become aggressive.
12. Always introduce dogs by taking them for a walk in neutral territory. Never bring a dog inside another dog's house before having them meet outside and walk together.
13. Lock your gates. Dogs are stolen out of yards every day.

ACKNOWLEDGEMENTS

Special thanks to my writing teacher, author Linzi Glass, cofounder of the Forgotten Dog Foundation, who helped shape this book. And to our writing group, L.J. Williamson, Margaret Byrne, Traude Gomez Rhine, and Susan Priver. Big thanks to my editors: Rand Lee, David R. Walker and Flo Selfman. And to my friends Victoria Burrows of Starpaws Rescue, Eldad Hagar of Hope for Paws, and Suzanna Urszuly and Steve Spiro who now head START Rescue. Steve and I have written "S.O.S.," a one-hour television drama about the rescue world and we are working with producer Alison Eastwood to get it on the air in the near future. An enormous thank you to the wonderful people who have fostered for me: Julia Flint, Deidre and Brad White, Ann Hesen, Eric Homan, John and Cece Teahan, Lynn Roth, Jennifer Clatfelter, Nathalie Kerkhove, Eric Rahier, Chelsey Forrey, Phil Miller, Jennifer Lyons, Ellen Gerstein, Jan Reesman, Sabi, and Ryan McDermott. Thank you Larry Hodges for hauling; Von and Euphoria Pet Salon for grooming; Sharp Pet Hospital; Noreen Reardon, my rescue mentor, and Bonnie Lambert, Paula Pizzi, and Justine Eyre for insight and support. But mostly, thank you to my husband, Jude Ciccolella—without him this book wouldn't exist, and these animals would not have been rescued.

Sammy & Sylva Cover Photo: Michael Brian
Author Photo: Dennis Apergis
Mazie Photo and Photo Editing: Vic Polizos
Tee & Frank Photo: Gilad Koriski
Allison & Addie Photo: Xanthe Elbrick

How You Can Help

- Volunteer at your local shelter or rescue group.
- Be the change you want to see. Petition in your area to get laws changed.
- Foster a dog or cat if you can.
- Call animal control if you see an animal being abused, neglected, or left in a hot car.
- Always keep an ID tag on your animal and get him/her microchipped.
- Spread the word about spay and neuter. A cat can have up to five litters in one year with six or more kittens in each litter. If you imagine that the baby kittens are not fixed either, you get an idea of why there is such an overpopulation of cats. Dogs can have, on average, six puppies per litter and have three litters a year. That's why spaying and neutering is so important.
- Always adopt from a shelter or rescue group. If people stop buying dogs from pet stores, puppy mills will eventually go out of business.
- You too can save a life!

If you would like to make a tax deductible donation to help the animals, please go to any of these sites:

www.TheForgottenDog.org
www.HopeForPaws.org
www.STARTrescue.org
www.StarPawsRescue.org
www.Billfoundation.org

CPSIA information can be obtained at www.ICGtesting.com
Printed in the USA
LVOW06*1827281115

464510LV00004B/21/P